CONSERVATION BY THE PEOPLE

ARTHUR HERBERT RICHARDSON

Conservation by the People:
the history of the conservation
movement in Ontario to 1970

PUBLISHED BY THE UNIVERSITY OF TORONTO PRESS
FOR THE CONSERVATION AUTHORITIES OF ONTARIO

© University of Toronto Press 1974
Toronto and Buffalo
Printed in Canada

ISBN 0-8020-3329-6
LC 74-77741

Photographic credits: Metropolitan Toronto and Region Conservation Authority, pages 4, 7 (top), 46, 47 (top), 51, 61, 71 (top), 75, 81, 96, 97, 124, 125, 130; Cannon, page 5; *London Free Press*, pages 6 (bottom), 118; Ministry of Natural Resources, page 7 (bottom); Department of Planning and Development, pages 8, 15, 32, 40, 54, 55, 60, 64 (bottom), 65, 87, 89, 90, 93, 106, 122, 123, 128; Royal Ontario Museum, page 11 (top); Norfolk London, page 11 (bottom); Ashley & Crippen, page 12 (top); Canadian Military, page 12 (bottom); University of Toronto, page 13; A.S.L. Barnes, pages 30, 57; Mrs Ellen Kripps, page 31; Lockwood Survey Corp. Ltd., page 33; Hunting Survey Corp. Ltd., page 34; Ron Nelson, page 77 (bottom); Junction Creek Conservation Authority, page 47 (bottom); Saugeen Valley Conservation Authority, pages 50, 64 (top), 71 (bottom); Ausable Conservation Authority Photo, pages 63, 131; North Grey Region Conservation Authority, page 72; Photographic Survey Corp. Ltd., pages 77, 101; Fred Muscat, page 80; Upper Thames River Conservation Authority, page 107.

Contents

Illustrations

Foreword

This publication is not merely a history of the conservation authorities in Ontario; it is a history of the development of the whole conservation movement which arose from the deep concern of many people for the condition of all the renewable natural resources in Ontario. These people realized that it was no longer possible to deal with resources separately or in a piecemeal fashion. All resources – water, land, forests, wildlife and recreation – must be considered at the same time and handled through a coordinated programme of resources management.

It was the Guelph Conference of 1941 which brought these early conservationists together and, as a result of its deliberations and recommendations, the government of Ontario established the Conservation Branch in 1944 and passed the Conservation Authorities Act in 1946.

Dr Arthur Herbert Richardson was the first director of the branch and Dr G. Ross Lord (formerly the chairman of the Metropolitan Toronto and Region Conservation Authority) was engaged from the beginning as consultant in hydraulic engineering.

Following Dr Richardson's retirement in 1961, the Committee of Conservation Authority Chairmen asked him, because of his intimate, first-hand knowledge, to write the history of the conservation movement in Ontario which he entitled *Conservation by the People*.

A.S.L. Barnes is a forester who worked under Dr Richardson in the Department of Lands and Forests in the 1930s. In 1941, when Mr Barnes was in uniform, he met Dr Richardson in Ottawa. Mr Barnes relates that Dr Richardson said to him: 'I wish I could get you out of the army, Alf, to work on the Ganaraska survey.' On his discharge in 1945, Barnes was made head of the forestry section of the Conservation Branch. He later was promoted to assistant director and on Dr Richardson's retirement became director, in which capacity he served from 1961 to 1970.

Dr Richardson completed the manuscript of this history before his death on 27 December 1971. As Dr Richardson was not familiar with the details of the work undertaken by the authorities during the last nine years, the Committee of Chairmen requested Mr Barnes and Dr Lord to review and edit the manuscript; this resulted in a number of additions, but alterations in the text have been kept to a minimum.

This history is published under the auspices of all the conservation authorities in Ontario.

C.G. CASWELL
CHAIRMAN OF THE CHAIRMEN'S COMMITTEE
OF ONTARIO CONSERVATION AUTHORITIES
SUDBURY, 1974

Introduction

It has often been said that the conservation authority movement in Ontario is unique on this continent, perhaps the world. This is probably true, and reading *Conservation by the People*, we can begin to understand why.

It has been pointed out that the movement began in the early thirties with the formation of interested groups such as the Ontario Conservation and Reforestation Association and the Federation of Ontario Naturalists. Many members of these groups were professionals and dedicated laymen who loved nature with a love that was above self-interest and strong enough to motivate them to action.

Ostensibly, the reason for pressing for conservation planning in the early forties was to provide useful and productive work for the men who would be returning to civilian life from World War II. No one could have foreseen that a surge in industrial development would look after these men adequately and that very few of them actually would be employed in conservation work. Regardless, the pressures for conservation planning were well founded and necessary. It was fortunate that there were capable and dedicated men in Ontario who lent their prestige, intelligence and energies to the forwarding of this work. While many concerned citizens gave strong support, it was fortunate that the government of Ontario was foresighted enough to gather professional staff of outstanding quality and competence to guide the conservation movement through its formative, growing years. Such names as Langford, Richardson, Barnes, Latornell, Bush, Murray, Blake, Mayall and others, call to mind an array of talent and competence which augured well for the more than twenty-five years of conservation development that followed.

While almost everyone agreed that conservation was a deserving endeavour, it took the ravaging calamity of Hurricane Hazel to shock governments, municipalities and citizens into action. Flood control became a vital concern, and since it was a part of conservation, the whole movement surged forward. Since the passing of the Conservation Authorities Act in 1946, the number of authorities in Ontario has grown to thirty eight. The success of conservation authorities has resulted from sound basic thinking and shrewd planning in the formative years. The initial concepts were simple, but so fundamentally right that only minor adjustments have been necessary. The basic ideas were three in number.

1/ *Local initiative* A conservation authority in any area could only be formed when the desires of the residents reached the point where they were willing to request the government of Ontario to form an authority. In making the request, the local people had to face up to the responsibility of contributing financially to the works of the authority and also agree to assume the burden of running the corporate body known as the conservation authority. This latter task involved burdens and responsibilities similar to the running of a municipality. The local initiative requirement meant that people living close to the problems were required to recognize and solve them. It also meant that solutions would not be imposed from above and an authority would only undertake those plans which it could face economically, culturally and democratically.

2/ *Cost sharing* The Conservation Authorities Act laid down that the costs of projects should be shared by the municipalities in the authority and by the provincial government. In time, cost sharing resolved itself into 50 percent by the authority and 50 percent by the government of Ontario. This proved to be one of the soundest ideas in the authority movement. It has meant that an authority can flourish only when the local people have enough enthusiasm and conviction to support it financially. It has also meant that the authority does not exceed the financial resources of its jurisdiction.

3/ *Watershed jurisdiction* Conservation authorities were to have jurisdiction over one or more watersheds. This stewardship was to cover all aspects of conservation in the area. This has meant that a conservation authority has been able to handle such problems as flood control in a complete and rational basis. By its power to establish regulations, an authority has been able to protect river valleys from building encroachment and erosion problems.

Conservation authorities have proved to be flexible agencies in their ability to promote and develop conservation works consistent with local topography and development patterns. In these respects, no two authorities are exactly alike. In metropolitan regions, authorities have had to concentrate on flood control, flood-plain planning, erosion control and provision of conservation areas for large populations; more rural authorities have enjoyed the challenge of reasonably-priced reforestation lands, wildlife and source areas developments.

Over the years, since 1950, a group known as the chairmen's committee, consisting of all of the authority chairmen, has made a great contribution by coordinating the efforts of all authorities and interpreting the viewpoint of these bodies for the government of Ontario. The first chairman of this committee was Oliver J. Wright of the Grand Valley Conservation Authority, followed by Gordon Pittock of the Upper Thames Valley Conservation Authority. The present chairman is Colin Caswell of the Junction Creek Conservation Authority. The chairmen's committee has given strong leadership by speaking with one voice to governments and the public in all matters of concern to authorities.

The conservation authorities movement has shown itself capable of expanding and developing to meet changing requirements and conditions. One evidence of this capacity has been the undertaking of lakeshore development by several authorities, as well as leadership in outdoor education for the young. It has been said that we are passing through the present into the future so quickly that we tend to forget the past. Many authorities have given thought to the richness of the past by preserving its treasures in pioneer villages and historic sites. While the achievements of conservation have been great in the past twenty-five years, the cost has been reasonable, indeed; in 1970, the Conservation Authorities Branch budget was $16 million for the support of thirty-eight authorities, about $1.40 per capita of people in the watersheds. I can think of no one more qualified to tell the story of the conservation movement in this province than the late Dr A.H. Richardson who, for seventeen years between 1944 and 1961, was the chief conservation engineer of the Ontario Department of Planning and Development. In that time Dr Richardson more than earned for himself the nickname 'Mr Conservation.'

The work of conservation will never end. Perhaps most conservationists are men of whom the prophet Joel wrote: 'Your old men shall dream dreams, your young men shall see visions.' Perhaps conservationists will always be setting aside lands so that they will not be all absorbed by the throbbing life of urban expansion, so that always some lands will be retained as oases of peace for those who toil in the city, so that in the years to come these valleys may echo with the laughter of children, so that young people may witness the ever-recurring miracle of spring, and so that parents may enjoy the solace of nature for tired bodies and minds.

G. ROSS LORD
FORMER CHAIRMAN, MTRCA

Acknowledgements

I am indebted to A.S.L. Barnes and the staff of the Conservation Authorities Branch for the material and statistics covering the period from 1961 to 1970 and specifically to K.M. Mayall who wrote Chapter 6. In addition I wish to acknowledge information provided by the Federation of Ontario Naturalists, the Ontario Department of Lands and Forests and the Ontario legislative library. I also wish to express my gratitude for the help tendered by Professor A.W. Baker, the late Professor A.F. Coventry, the late J.D. Thomas and C.R. Purcell in refreshing my memory of some of the events of a quarter of a century ago. In conclusion I would be remiss if I did not express my gratitude to the thousands of people, too numerous to name individually, who have served as members of the conservation authorities and their advisory boards with a devotion beyond the call of duty. Their works and accomplishments will stand as monuments to their dedication which this history endeavours to outline.

A.H. RICHARDSON

CONSERVATION BY THE PEOPLE

I
The Gestation of an Idea

When the Honourable Dana Porter, Ontario minister of planning and development, decided in 1944 to establish a Conservation Branch in his department, it was
with the realization that the time was opportune to embark on a programme of
conservation in which the municipalities and the government of Ontario should
work as partners. With the establishment of this branch the conservation authorities movement in Ontario was born.

It should be stated, however, that the decision of the minister at this time was not
precipitant but the result of many years of sincere concern that more should be
done to preserve and save the province's natural resources. This concern exhibited
itself in many ways but the most important efforts were initiated by a group of
organizations which existed or came into being during the decade prior to 1940. Of
this group the Federation of Ontario Naturalists and the Ontario Conservation and
Reforestation Association were especially zealous; because of this fine leadership,
their activities will be recorded at some length.

Interest in natural history in Ontario has been promoted, to a large extent, by
men and women who became interested in this fascinating study as an avocation.
As a result, many of these 'amateurs' were joined by professionals and, working
together formed naturalists clubs; in some cases the club had been named after a
member who was outstanding in some specialized field of nature study.

In 1931 there was a number of these clubs scattered throughout Ontario, each
carrying on its own programme with no formal attachment to each other. Realizing
that a federation of nature clubs was desirable, so that concerted action could be
taken on matters such as governmental legislation affecting wildlife, the question of
a union of these clubs was proposed at a meeting of the Brodie Club, which was the
senior natural history club in Toronto, held 3 February 1931. Professor J.R.
Dymond introduced a proposal designed to enable the clubs to formulate collective
policies and to provide the machinery whereby these policies might be implemented, and to stimulate a more general appreciation of the educational and
aesthetic value of wildlife on the part of the general public.

After investigation by an organizing committee, a general meeting of the Federation of Ontario Naturalists (FON) was held in Hart House, Toronto, on 15 May 1931. W.E. Saunders of London, Ontario, was elected president and Professor A.F. Coventry, secretary-treasurer. W.E. Saunders was the logical choice for this position because he combined a breadth of interest with thoroughness of knowledge and a warm personality that made him the outstanding naturalist of his time in Ontario. He continued as president until his death in 1942 at the age of 82.

The charter clubs of the federation were: the Brodie Club of Toronto, the Biological Club of Toronto, the McIlwraith Ornithological Club of London, the Kent Nature Club of Chatham, the Hamilton Protection Society, the Queen's Natural History Society, Kingston and the Toronto Field-Naturalist Club.

From this modest beginning in 1931 with seven affiliate clubs and a few hundred members, the federation has grown over the years until in 1970 its membership was composed of 45 affiliate clubs, 8,000 adult members, 900 student members and 22,000 young naturalists. It also publishes three excellent periodicals: *The Ontario Naturalist*, four times a year; the *Young Naturalist*, ten times a year and the *Newsletter*, five times a year.

It is not possible to pay adequate tribute, in a few sentences, to the fine work which has been done over the years by this organization. By using a multiplicity of attractive methods, especially field activities, the federation has had an incalculable impact on the thinking of the people of this province in the cause of conservation. One important project initiated by its members was the report on 'The Natural Resources of King Township, Ontario, 1938,' an area of approximately 140 square miles about twenty miles north-northwest of Toronto. The purpose of the survey is best stated in an introductory note by the late Aubrey Davis of Newmarket – a town in the area – who not only sponsored the survey, but contributed the funds to carry it out.

The survey of King Township was prompted by my memories of the different and more pleasant township of my boyhood days fifty years ago. Since those days, the township has become progressively impoverished, the deterioration being most marked during the last ten years. A belief that this deterioration could be halted led me to consult men who had for years been interested in conservation, and as a result, the committee named in the report was formed.

The course decided upon was to make a survey of the past and present conditions in the township, and to use this as a basis of a plan of rehabilitation work that would command the attention of all the older provinces. It was hoped to restore the township to a state in which the renewable natural resources – trees, crops and wildlife, together with its water and soil – might recover during the next twenty years or so a large measure of their earlier vigour, and this without more than the initial expenditure of time and money needed to create stable conditions.

It was expected that the work, as outlined in the plan, would be so carried out, under expert guidance, as to give a body of unemployed young men of more than average intelligence, a training which would equip them for employment as key men in similar projects in other places, while at the same time it conferred permanent benefits on King Township.

The report shows beyond question the need for active rehabilitation measures; the plan for these is simple; its execution requires only the cooperation of all authorities and organizations concerned.

The survey was carried out by Kenneth M. Mayall from April 1937 to January 1938. He was also responsible for writing the report and the preparation of the maps which it contained.

A plan was prepared for improvement of the township and the work to be undertaken in the first year: Planting 400 acres in trees, drilling several test wells, building small dams, establishing of small tree nurseries, educating school children in conservation generally and, in particular, erosion control and cooperative wildlife management.

The estimated cost of the first year's operation was $12,000. Representation was made to the government of Canada and the government of Ontario for the funds, but both governments refused. However, the government of Ontario offered to provide without charge the necessary 483,000 trees for reforestation.

Although the rehabilitation of the area selected was not carried out as the report recommended, the King Township survey was nevertheless a forward step in conservation methods in Ontario, because it spearheaded the concept that conservation cannot be attained by piecemeal methods, but rather that it must be accomplished with a multi-purpose programme for the renewal of *all* natural resources in an area.

Hard on the heels of the King Township report and the enthusiasm it engendered came support from another source, the ocra – the Ontario Conservation and Reforestation Association.

The association had been formed in January 1936 and while many individuals contributed to its success during eighteen years of activity, the spearhead of the group was Watson H. Porter, managing editor of the *Farmer's Advocate* magazine of London, Ontario. Of the genesis of the organization, Porter had written:

[Who can forget] the exceedingly dry season of 1936 when hundreds of farm folk all along the front of old Ontario were drawing water for domestic use and for their livestock. It was pitiful to see cattle milling around dried-up water holes and going daily to the stream bottoms where always previously there was water. Wells that never failed before went dry, springs dried up. The situation indeed was serious and one could see that the ill effects of drought had been intensified by the needless slaughter of trees and the denudation of the countryside. It was obvious that something should be done.

Early in the autumn of 1936 the Rotary Club of Simcoe invited representatives from several surrounding counties and at a special dinner meeting stressed the need of some concerted action to halt the mad destruction of tree growth. Monroe Landon and the Norfolk County Chamber of Commerce had been sounding the warning bell for several years and the county council was already then embarked on a reforestation programme. The meeting agreed that time for action had come and that one county could not accomplish very much alone. The wooded areas and swamps in one county feed the streams that flow through adjoining counties, it was pointed out, and real progress could be made only when

Dr A.H. Richardson, director, Conservation Branch, 1944–61

municipalities all over the province united in forward-looking conservation policy actually put into effect.

An article entitled 'A New Reforestation Policy for Ontario,' was published in the *Farmer's Advocate*, under date of 10 September 1936, and this brought forth considerable comment from many different quarters of the province. It was becoming increasingly apparent that Southwestern Ontario, at any rate, was ready for some kind of a conservation programme, but the problem was to get it organized. Individuals had been preaching reforestation and conservation for almost fifty years, but, as Mark Twain said about the weather, 'nobody did anything about it.' It was suggested on several occasions and by different parties, that an attempt should be made to unite all these people favourable to conservation into some kind of an organization, and it was agreed from the start that it must be a rural movement. If the farm people and the officers of rural municipalities would not put their shoulders to the wheel, then it would not be worthwhile going any further. Consequently, an invitation was sent out to the nine counties in this southwestern peninsula to meet in the agricultural office, London, on December 17, 1936. The response was most gratifying. The wardens of six of the nine counties were present and the other three sent representatives. All the agricultural representatives were in attendance; officers of the Forestry Branch of the Ontario Department of Lands and Forests and of the Department of Agriculture were there to serve in any capacity where they were needed, as were members of the press. The meeting bespoke a keen interest in conservation and the movement was launched.

In order to expedite business and keep the delegates together for the entire session, Ernest Weld, manager of the William Weld Company, entertained them at luncheon. Then they broke up into half a dozen different committees and drafted the programme and policies that officers of the movement have since attempted to put into effect.

The meeting at London gave evidence of a genuine interest throughout the countryside and it was decided that other counties were no doubt just as ready to proceed along the same

A.S.L. Barnes, director, Conservation
Authorities Branch, 1961–70

lines. Consequently, a meeting was called at the Ontario Agricultural College, Guelph, on 13 January 1937 for the remaining thirteen counties west of Toronto, and here again the response was highly favourable. Meetings were also held at Bowmanville and Kemptville with the result that more than one hundred men, representing all portions of old Ontario, had some part in shaping the policy and programme of what became the OCRA.

It was agreed that the province should be divided into five zones with the county committees in each zone setting up an executive of their own. The three officers of each zone committee automatically became members of the provincial committee of fifteen, which was known as the Ontario Conservation and Reforestation Association.

Copies of the recommendations approved by the committees at London, Guelph and Bowmanville were sent to all the county councils in Ontario at their January session in 1937. The newly drafted programme was widely approved by these local governments and since that time their support has been one of the most pleasing features of the whole movement.

All those associated with the initial efforts will not forget the splendid assistance given by the press of Ontario. From the start the press has been consistent and most generous in its advocacy of conservation.

The OCRA was a unique organization; it did not have a constitution, there was no membership list, no membership fees, and no salaries or honorariums, and no expenses were paid to any officials. It drew its membership largely from the reforestation and agricultural committees of the counties but anyone was welcome to attend. For the financing of meetings, tours, field days and the printing of literature it received annual grants from the counties of Ontario. As its membership was composed largely of municipal officials, it was in a strong position to influence the government regarding conservation matters. During its life it was instrumental in

Honourable Dana Porter, first minister
Ontario Department of Planning and
Development, 1944–48

Dr G.B. Langford, director, Ontario
Department of Planning and Development, 1944–46

bringing about many needy improvements regarding the natural resources of
Southern Ontario.

J.D. Thomas was elected vice-president because 'I was intrigued by the enthusiasm of the meeting, and because I talked too much.' With the approval and
cooperation of Dr E.J. Zavitz, chief of the reforestation division, Department of
Lands and Forests, the division staff assisted the association in many ways,
particularly in planning programmes and loaning equipment for field days.

Dr G. Ross Lord, consultant in hydraulic engineeering for conservation authorities, 1944–70, and chairman of the Metropolitan Toronto and Region Conservation Authority, 1958–1973.

Kenneth M. Mayall, director of the King Township survey in 1937–38, and author of the resulting report.

The method of arousing interest in conservation throughout Southern Ontario was chiefly by well-planned field days and conservation tours. These tours usually took a whole day and in many cases included an itinerary of more than one hundred miles. Such a tour included inspection of reforestation projects, farm planning, pollution, water problems and woodlot management. Lunch was usually served en route under canvas with appropriate speakers, and a dinner was held at night, with speakers or an illustrated talk. For most of these all-day tours the programme was

The executive committee of the Ontario Conservation and Reforestation Association, a prime proponent of conservation practices in the province, held its last meeting before the organization disbanded on 16 May 1957. The executive was, back row, left to right: H.F. Crown; A.H. Richardson; and L.N. Johnson. Middle row: F.L. Weldon, Lindsay; W.H. Hunter, Orangeville; L. Osborne, Paris; Angus Smith, Mt Forest; Theo Parker, Mono Mills; M. McDonough. Branchton; R.C. Banbury, Brighton; A.S.L. Barnes; and F. Stewart, Hamilton. Front row: Victor Purvis, Mallorytown; N.A. Fletcher, Hannon; T.A. Wilson, chairman, Pakenham; H. McBeth, Salford; Percy Gooding, Hilton; and M.H. Johnson, Peterborough.

described in a pocket-size mimeographed book of approximately fifty pages; in addition to the map showing the itinerary, the booklet contained a description of all important conservation projects in the area with suitable illustrations. Some of these field days were planned particularly for school children, in which case the outing was held in a county forest; the children in the immediate area would travel from their school to the forest for instruction, and on several of these conservation picnics the attendance exceeded 1,000.

To increase the interest in conservation among school children, the association published a bulletin entitled *School Forestry Clubs*, which was widely distributed by the association; an additional 20,000 copies were sent by the Ontario Department of Education to all schools in Ontario. Also, during the life of the association, a printed record of its activities was published two or three times a year.

Between 1936 and 1954 when the association was active, much progress was made in Southern Ontario in coming to grips with conservation problems: a soils department was created at the Ontario Agricultural College; as a result of the Guelph Conference, the Ganaraska survey was carried out; a Conservation Branch was established in the newly formed Department of Planning and Development; the Conservation Authorities Act was passed by the legislature and several authorities established; the Trees Conservation Act was passed; two new tree nurseries were established; planting stock for reforestation increased from ten million trees in 1937 to seventeen million trees in 1940; district foresters were appointed for Southern Ontario; the Assessment Act was amended regarding assessment on reforested land; the report of the Select Committee of the Legislature on Conservation was tabled and printed; and lastly, the conservation-minded groups in Ontario led by Frank H. Kortright had formed the Conservation Council of Ontario.

The OCRA in no way claimed to be responsible for all these changes which took place during its lifetime, but during these years the association carried the banner of conservation, and carried it high, and many of these admirable advances in conservation were hastened – and some definitely brought to fruition – by the persistent efforts of OCRA members.

In the long catalogue of achievements of this association there is one which, because of its importance, will be dealt with separately.

At the annual meeting of the association held in Toronto on 24 February 1941 there was much discussion regarding the possibility of using returned soldiers for a comprehensive conservation programme in Ontario. The meeting passed this resolution:

Realizing the vital necessity of conserving our natural resources and appreciating the fact that Canada will be confronted with a vital problem of rehabilitation following present war,

Therefore be it resolved that this association appoint a committee to study the establishment of a Canadian conservation corps or other plans related to conservation and reforestation.

And be it further resolved that such a committee be appointed by the chair today with power to act, and that this committee proceed to secure the support and active cooperation of all other interested bodies.

The president named J.D. Thomas convenor of the committee and to work with him appointed Monroe Landon, Simcoe; W.H. Casselman, Chesterville; and A.H. Richardson, Toronto.

When the committee enquired into the interest of other groups in such a proposal, it discovered that the Federation of Ontario Naturalists at its annual meeting in Toronto on 11 February 1941 – two weeks before the annual meeting of the OCRA – had appointed a committee which in intent was the same as the one appointed by the OCRA. Acting together the two committees invited representatives from all organizations active in conservation to meet at the Ontario Agricultural College, Guelph, on 25 April 1941 to explore the possibilities of promoting such a conservation scheme. Those who attended were: Dr E.S. Archibald, Director, Experimental Farms Service, Ottawa; Professor A.W. Baker, Ontario Agricultural College, Guelph; Dr H.C. Bliss, Toronto; Dr J.F. Booth, Department of Agriculture, Ottawa; Professor J. Buchanan, OAC, Guelph; President G.I. Christie, OAC, Guelph; J. Coke, economics branch, Department of Agriculture, Ottawa; Professor A.F. Coventry, University of Toronto; Professor J.D. Detwiler, University of Western Ontario, London; Dr N.K. Douglas, Owen Sound; Professor W.M. Drummond,

OAC, Guelph; Professor J.R. Dymond, Royal Ontario Museum, Toronto; E.K. Hampson, Toronto; Professor J.E. Howitt, OAC, Guelph; Professor R.G. Knox, OAC, Guelph; Monroe Landon, Simcoe; Professor F.N. Marcellus, OAC, Guelph; Captain Thos. Magladery, New Liskeard; Professor T.F. McIlwraith, Royal Ontario Museum, Toronto; Professor G.P. McRostie, OAC, Guelph; Major J.B. Morrison, Fergus; W.H. Porter, London; C.R. Purcell, Men of the Trees, Toronto; A.H. Richardson, Department of Lands and Forests, Toronto; Dr C.B. Ross, Muskoka Hospital, Gravenhurst; Professor G.N. Rhunke, OAC, Guelph; J.D. Thomas, National Selective Service, Ottawa; W.H.J. Tisdale, Toronto; G.C. Toner, Royal Ontario Museum, Toronto; and C.A. Walkinshaw, Toronto.

The names of those attending this meeting held on the OAC campus that spring morning in 1941 was a roll call of the faithful in conservation. There was an atmosphere of optimism, but a sense of urgency also, at last something truly worthwhile could be accomplished, but it must be done quickly and well.

At the first meeting it was decided that the name of the group should be the Guelph Conference; J.D. Thomas was elected chairman and Professor J.R. Dymond, secretary-treasurer. The member organizations were: Ontario Conservation and Reforestation Association; Canadian Society of Forest Engineers (now the Canadian Institute of Forestry); Federation of Ontario Naturalists; Royal Canadian Institute; Canadian Society of Technical Agriculturalists; Canadian Conservation Association; Ontario Federation of Anglers and Hunters; Royal Canadian Legion; and Men of the Trees.

At a subsequent meeting the Guelph Conference agreed on these four major objectives:

1/To give coherence and coordination to a programme of conservation.
2/To make available to government or municipal bodies the advice and guidance of its members who are recognized as specialists in their respective fields.
3/To give impetus in every possible way to implementing recommendations regarding conservation measures.
4/To disseminate information relating to the present status of our renewable natural resources and the need for undertaking adequate measures for their restoration.

In order to adequately carry out and make known the four objectives the conference decided to publish a sixteen-page brochure. Professor A.F. Coventry consented to prepare the booklet which was entitled *Conservation and Post War Rehabilitation*.

Because of the importance of this document and what transpired following its publication, it is appropriate that the abstract of its contents be recorded:

This memorandum has been prepared in the belief that a programme of conservation can do a vital service to the province and at the same time contribute in an important degree to the national problem of re-establishing men in civil life after the war.

The present conditions of the renewable natural resources of agricultural Ontario are examined, and a plan is proposed for their improvement.

Dr J.R. Dymond, Royal Ontario Museum, secretary-treasurer of the Guelph Conference

Dr J.D. Detwiler, a pioneer of the conservation movement, led the fight for flood control on the Thames River in the 1930s and 1940s.

1/ *Existing conditions* These are discussed under the headings of: desiccation, floods, erosion, pollution of waters, forest cover, waste lands and swamps, soil management, wildlife, tourists, existing remedial measures.

2/ *Summary of present conditions* Present conditions may be fairly summarized by the statement that all the renewable natural resources of the province are in an unhealthy state. None of these natural resources will restore themselves under present conditions, and the

J.D. Thomas, chairman of the historic Guelph Conference, 1941, and long-time champion of conservation in Ontario.

Watson H. Porter, managing editor of the *Farmer's Advocate,* used the columns of his magazine to promote the cause of conservation and wise land management.

need for far-reaching measures of restoration and conservation is acute; without them, conditions will get progressively worse.

Small measures of restoration and conservation are being taken in most fields, but they are so small as to be insignificant in their effects, when compared with the magnitude of the need. To be effective, treatment must be province wide in plan.

3/ *Necessary action.* To arrest the degradation of natural resources and to restore in

Professor A.F. Coventry, professor of biology at the University of Toronto, served on several conservation committees and was instrumental in bringing many natural history clubs together in the Federation of Ontario Naturalists.

some measure their lost productivity involves replacing the unplanned individualistic exploitation of the past hundred years by planned management based on knowledge and recognizing public as well as private interest.

Natural resources form a delicate balanced system in which all parts are interdependent and they cannot be successfully handled, piecemeal. The present situation requires the coordination of existing relevant knowledge and its amplification where necessary, and then the development of a comprehensive plan for treating the natural resources on a wide public basis.

To this end a body of technically trained men should be appointed, with powers to use pertinent information, wherever available, to initiate field work where needed to complete the knowledge and to draw up a working plan of conservation, carrying on their task at all times in close co-operation with the administrative authorities.

4/ *Difficulties* It is clear that such a treatment of our natural resources cuts across traditional lines, both of opinion and administrative practice, but this must be faced in view of the gravity of the problem.

There will be a shortage of trained men to direct the projects, and steps will have to be taken to train more.

Both the difficulties and the magnitude of the problem emphasize the need for immediate action. The plan should be ready for application as soon as possible. The future welfare of the province depends on the maintenance of its natural resources; and Canada will be faced with the problem of re-establishing many men in civil life. A well-planned programme of conservation meets these demands in high degree.

About this time there was much concern regarding an economic slump which might occur following the war. Accordingly, the ground work was laid for a programme of useful employment for men returning from active service by many municipalities and other groups across the country. The federal government gave leadership to this apparent need by appointing the Advisory Committee on Reconstruction in 1941 under the chairmanship of Dr F. Cyril James, principal of McGill University. The terms of reference for this committee included 'to examine and discuss the post-war reconstruction and to make recommendations as to what governmental facilities should be established to deal with this question.'

One of the sub-committees appointed by the committee was charged 'to consider and recommend ... the policy and programme appropriate to the most effective conservation and maximum future development of the natural resources of the dominion of Canada, having regard to the importance of these resources as national assets and emphasizing the part which the proposed policies may play in providing employment opportunities at the end of the present war.' This sub-committee, on Conservation and Development of Natural Resources, functioned under the chairmanship of Dr R.C. Wallace, principal of Queen's University.

A committee of the Guelph Conference met with the Committee on Reconstruction in Ottawa in August, 1941. At this meeting the purpose of the Guelph Conference was outlined, and the need for a type of demonstration survey discussed. It was agreed that if an appropriate project could be outlined, to be conceived and executed as a special piece of conservation research for general application to Canada, the committee might request an appropriation to assist with the cost of such a study.

The chairman of the Guelph Conference, J.D. Thomas, discussed the proposals of the conference with Mitchell Hepburn, premier of Ontario in December of the same year. Mr Hepburn gave his support to the project and later requested the Honourable N.O. Hipel, minister of Lands and Forests to discuss it in further detail with members of the conference. Subsequently, the minister authorized the appointment of the Interdepartmental Committee on Conservation and Rehabilitation with A.H. Richardson, Forester, Department of Lands and Forests, as full-time chairman, and with powers to organize the survey. In addition to the chairman, the membership of the committee was: Professor A.W. Baker, head of the Department of Entomology, Ontario Agricultural College; Norman Davies, inspector of agricultural classes, Department of Education; Otto Holden, chief hydraulic engineer, Hydro-Electric Power Commission of Ontario; Dr M.E. Hurst, provincial geologist, Department of Mines; H.H. Mackay, director of fish culture and biologist, Department of Game and Fisheries; Dr J.T. Phair, chief medical officer of health, Department of Health; and Professor G.N. Ruhnke, head of the Department of Chemistry, Ontario Agricultural College.

The outcome of these negotiations was that a pilot survey would be carried out under the direction of the Ontario Interdepartmental Committee and be financed jointly by the two senior governments.

The early months of 1942 were spent making plans for spring. By May the selection of the area to be surveyed – a watershed of 103 square miles, drained by the Ganaraska River, which empties into Lake Ontario at the town of Port Hope – had been decided upon, and the necessary maps, aerial photographs and equipment

Acres of sand, barely tied down with grass cover and scrub trees, were typical of much of Southern Ontario in 1941 when the Ganaraska River watershed was studied and an historic report compiled.

had been secured. One urgent question was finding qualified men to do the work. Student assistance was not available because young men were enlisting in the armed forces. Accordingly, it was decided to use science teachers from the high schools and collegiates of the province.

However, there was still a lack of interest in the survey by some members of the Ontario government. Spring passed rapidly into the warm days of July but the green light had not been given. Finally, approval was received and the survey company numbering twenty-five men were notified to report at camp on 20 July. This left the remainder of July and the month of August to carry out the work from which a week, at least, had to be deducted for training the staff. Fortunately, however, many high school students were employed during the summer in essential work and the schools in Ontario did not open that year until 1 October.

Men of many different professions and levels of government were interested in the project, so a field day was held on the site on 18 September; by car and on foot they were shown the more interesting features of the watershed. Dr R.C. Wallace presided at the luncheon at which thirty four were in attendance.

The *Farmer's Advocate* reported, 'On 18 September a group of prominent officials directly responsible for and interested in the Ganaraska survey visited the watershed. The group gathered at the survey camp site which was situated on the upper part of the area adjacent to the Durham County Forest, and had lunch at noon, at which Dr R.C. Wallace, principal of Queen's University presided. Following lunch A.H. Richardson, chairman of the Interdepartmental Committee and under whose direction the survey had been conducted outlined briefly the purpose of the survey and explained that the gathering had been called in order that those directly responsible for the work might see the types of country included on the area and also get first hand information on the progress of the survey to date.'

Following the outline of the work the group was taken on a short motor trip to typical areas of the watershed. These included large areas of abandoned farm land; examples of wind, gully and sheet erosion; a cut-over stream valley; a source of one of the main branches of the Ganaraska; forest plantations; and a splendid example of natural woodland containing white pine, hemlock and mixed hardwood equal to any now privately owned in Southern Ontario.

Those in attendance were: Dr R.C. Wallace, principal of Queen's University and chairman of the sub-committee on natural resources, of the dominion Committee on Reconstruction; and the following members of the committee – John McLeish, former deputy minister of mines, Ottawa; D.A. McDonald, associate dominion forester, Ottawa; Professor Esdras Minville, University of Montreal; Dr J.J. O'Neill, dean of the Graduate School, McGill University, Montreal – Dr L.C. Marsh, research adviser, Ottawa; J.E. McKay, secretary of the dominion Committee on Reconstruction, Ottawa. Members of the Ontario Interdepartmental Committee attending were Dr M.E. Hurst, provincial geologist, Department of Mines, Toronto; Norman Davies, inspector of agricultural classes, Department of Education, Toronto; Professors G.M. Ruhnke and A.W. Baker, Ontario Agricultural College, Guelph; H.H. McKay, biologist and director of Fish Culture Branch, Department of Game and Fisheries, Toronto; and Dr J.T. Phair, Department of Health, Toronto. Other guests were: Dr L.B. Williams, Men of the Trees, Toronto; W.R. Reek, deputy minister of agriculture, Toronto; H.C. Rickaby, deputy minister of mines, Toronto; H.R. Hare, Ottawa; Professor John Detwiler, Department of Biology, University of Western Ontario, London; James Rennie, Ontario Conservation and Reforestation Association, Toronto; C. Hooper, chairman, reforestation committee, County of York, Toronto; R.A. Bryce, president, Canadian Institute of Mines and Metallurgy, Toronto; J.D. Thomas, chairman of the Guelph Conference, Ottawa; Vernon Johnson, Canadian International Paper Company, Montreal; E.A. Summer, agricultural representative, Bowmanville; Professor J.R. Dymond, Royal Ontario Museum, Toronto; A. Gosselin, Ottawa; L.R. Webber, Guelph; A.L. Willis, Guelph; Professor F.F. Morwick, Guelph; J. Cope, senior economist, Department of Agriculture, Ottawa; G.M. Linton, superintendent the Orono nursery; Dr C.T. Currelly, Royal Ontario Museum, Toronto; E.J. Zavitz, chief, reforestation division, Toronto. Representatives of the *Canadian Statesman*, Bowmanville, the *Globe and Mail*, Toronto, and the *Port Hope Guide* were also in attendance.

The work of compiling the report, including maps and photographs, was done during the fall of 1942 and the spring of 1943. In this work Verschoyle B. Blake, Muriel Miller and the Interdepartmental Committee, which met monthly from October 1942 until May the following year, were of great assistance. The report was typewritten in six copies, and contained 450 pages, legal size, original photographs, maps and graphs, all suitably bound. The first copy was delivered to the office of the minister of lands and forests on 15 June 1943.

The following are excerpts from Dr Wallace's introduction to the Ganaraska report:

The area through which the Ganaraska River runs is approximately one hundred square miles in extent. Around the Port Hope area, where the river empties into Lake Ontario, there are still flourishing farms. But a great part of the headwaters is today a barren waste. Its prosperous days of lumbering, settlement and substantial contribution to Canadian wealth are merely history, although history that is all too recent in terms of the exploitation and exhaustion of resources. While the major purposes of the survey were to determine how a balanced redevelopment of the resources of the watershed area could be carried through, it has seemed valuable, in order to point the lesson of the lack of conservation, to recapitulate some of this history.

The principal work of analyzing the resources was undertaken as comprehensively as possible. Thanks to the contributions of the various specialists, the surveys extend to climate, soils, vegetation, forestry, physical and economic aspects of agriculture, plant diseases, entomology, wildlife, waterflow and utilization. The result is that the report includes scientific data of types not usually included in routine survey reports.

The practical conclusions of the report were that in the Ganaraska area a rehabilitation programme could be carried out which would provide work for 600 men for a period of approximately two years. The projects would include woodlot improvement, tree planting, erosion control, dam construction, the organization of recreational centres and farm improvement. What applied to this area applied in a general way to other areas of a similar kind. The report was, therefore, taken as a type report, of general significance for the conservation and rehabilitation of all our resources throughout Canada.

The report was not designed solely for the specialist. It did not content itself with facts and figures, but presented the cause and effect of changes in the area in an illuminating way. A liberal number of illustrations supplement the text; in themselves they told a story of unwise settlement and land use, and the urgent necessity for rehabilitation. It was hoped that this contribution to our literature on conservation would bear good fruit, both in stimulating public interest and in developing programmes ready for action.

The following appreciation of the report was written by Professor J.R. Dymond, secretary-treasurer of the Guelph Conference:

The results of the survey of the Ganaraska River basin and recommendations based thereon, have recently been published in a report which may well become a landmark in Ontario conservation literature. The form of the Ganaraska report is in strong contrast to that of the usual government reports. Its numerous illustrations and general attractive appearance add greatly to its educational value. The federal and Ontario governments who are responsible for the publication of the information contained in the Ganaraska report in such attractive form are to be warmly commended. The general subject covered by the report – the condition of the soil, water, woods, wildlife, etc of a particular area of agricultural Ontario and recommendations for its restoration based on exact knowledge – is one vital to the future welfare of our province. It is therefore of importance that this first report be presented in such a way that it will reach and be understood by as many interested people as possible.

Many compliments have been bestowed on the Ganaraska report, but the one cherished most was made by the Honourable Dana Porter. He held the report high in his hand and said in his affable manner, 'Mr Richardson, this is a classic.'

A report, to have any practical value, must have a number of specific recommendations. The preparing of these for the Ganaraska report was one of the chief concerns of the Interdepartmental Committee. As a result, the report carried 25 recommendations covering legislation, employment, surveys and records. It is not necessary to comment on all of these but one which has a direct bearing on the conservation authorities should be mentioned.

Recommendation No. 2 stated that: 'Legislation be enacted combining the best features of the Grand River Conservation Commission and the Muskingum Watershed Conservancy District, Ohio, so that municipalities in any part of Ontario may undertake a similar conservation programme.' The implementation of this recommendation by the government of Ontario produced the Conservation Authorities Act in 1946.

There had been many conservation surveys in Ontario over the years and many other approaches to the government for a new look at the problems of conservation, but it is sad to relate few have been acted upon. But the Ganaraska survey, while repeating many of the things which had been dealt with in other reports, but with a new approach, included useful and healthy work for men whom the government was anxious to assist in the readjustment period following the war.

In retrospect some may consider that the Ganaraska survey did not accomplish one of the primary purposes for which it was organized – the rehabilitation of returned soldiers following the second world war. But it was not the fault of the sponsors that this part of the project did not materialize. However, the main thrust of the report – a new and comprehensive approach to conservation in Southern Ontario – emerged with vigour and new enthusiasm.

Furthermore, it was remarkable that this scheme was accepted and financed jointly by the two senior governments during months of heavy strain on the part of the Canadian people. The country was not only at war, but at the time the survey was carried out the war was reaching a period of precariousness which lay heavily on the minds of the free world, especially Great Britain and the commonwealth nations.

During the spring of 1944, Dr Leonard Marsh, of the reconstruction committee of the federal government, and the author, collaborated in abridging the report for the printer, after which it was released for distribution early in the summer.

The Interdepartmental Committee had now ceased to meet and was disbanded in 1945. Soon the war was over in Europe and by early autumn the great ships were crowded with men returning to their homeland. No action, however, had been taken by either government to plan for the implementation of recommendations of the Ganaraska report.

2

The Roots Sink Deeply

In 1944 Premier George A. Drew of Ontario decided to establish a new ministry within his government, the Department of Planning and Development, to resolve certain urgent problems of the time – one of which was conservation. His thinking on this subject can best be explained by quoting excerpts from an address which the premier delivered at the convention of conservation in Southern Ontario in Toronto, 29–30 November 1946. Although the remarks were made after the new department had been established, they indicate his reasons for considering conservation when the proposed new department was taking form in his mind two years earlier.

I think that perhaps I might deal with one aspect of planning and conservation which it seems to me is fundamental to the approach that we make to this whole problem. Conservation, such as is set forth in the list of activities of this conference, is planning of a very high order, and it seems to me it is essential that we decide just what kind of planning for conservation – or for anything else – it is that we want.

Speaking as the head of the government in this province, which must, after all, assume some responsibility, and which seeks to cooperate in this activity as much as possible, may I say most definitely that our concept of planning is that we should make sure that the local municipal bodies, and the voluntary organizations within the municipal areas, retain and exercise full control over their own affairs. We base that upon a very simple and, I hope, not misguided belief, that the closer government is to the people the better and more economical is that government. After all, our whole system of development in this country has grown up from the strong basis of local government and from the direct contact of people in each community with their own affairs.

I believe the planning for conservation which is proceeding with a very high degree of vision and with very real hopes of a broad field of achievement, if that is to go ahead on a truly democratic basis, then I think it must go ahead upon the voluntary cooperation of all the component municipal units that are within that area and within any area with which we are dealing, and that the time has not yet come for local governments, to abdicate their authority to provincial governments, nor, shall I say, for provincial governments to abdicate their authority to a still more remote central government.

There is much restoration to be done, as well as conservation, but it can be done, and with a long-term vision and with planning as to the type of community we desire, there is no reason at all why we cannot restore those natural advantages which nature has endowed us with so generously.

At the session of the legislature 1944, the Department of Planning and Development Act was passed, the most important section of which reads:

3/ The minister shall collaborate with the ministers having charge of the departments of the public service of Ontario, the Ministers having charge of the departments of the public service of the dominion and of other provinces, with municipal councils, with agricultural, industrial, labour, mining, trade and other associations and organizations and with public and private enterprise with a view to formulating plans to create, assist, develop and maintain productive employment and to develop the human and material resources of the province and to that end shall coordinate the work and functions of the departments of the public service of Ontario.

On 8–9 May 1944 the premier called a conference in Toronto to discuss problems of planning and development. At this meeting he announced that Dana Porter, MLA for St. George's riding in the city of Toronto, had been appointed minister of the new department and that arrangements had been made with the University of Toronto to loan Dr George B. Langford, professor of mining geology to serve as director of the department. At that time, director was a position in the civil service senior to deputy minister and this title was used to place him in a favourable position when coordinating the work and functions of other departments.

During the summer of 1944 the Honourable Dana Porter and Dr Langford spent the best part of a week visiting the Tennessee Valley Authority. The TVA chairman at that time was David E. Lillianthal – a dynamic personality – who was courtesy personified in describing the purpose and progress of the authority.

I write of the Tennessee Valley [Lillianthal had explained in defining his vision of TVA] but all this could have happened in almost any of a thousand other valleys where rivers run from the hills to the sea. For the valleys of the earth have these things in common; the water, the air, the land, the minerals, the forests. In Brazil and in the Argentine, in China and in India, in Canada and the United States, there are just such rivers, rivers flowing through mountain canyons, through agricultural land, through barren wastes – rivers that in the violence of flood menace the land and the people, then sulk in idleness and drought – rivers all over the world waiting to be controlled by men.

While the Tennessee Valley Authority is administratively and financially quite different from the type of authority which was envisioned for Ontario – TVA being supported wholly by the United States government – it demonstrated the need, that all natural resources must be treated as a combined resource development. This was the basic fact, already widely promulgated in Ontario, that the minister and the director brought back from the Tennessee Valley Authority.

To assist the government in formulating plans for the Ganaraska watershed, which it was expected would be the first authority to be formed, the Ganaraska Advisory Board was appointed by order-in-council 18 August 1944 with the following members: Frederick Bowen, Newcastle, chairman; Herbert K. Long, Port Hope, secretary; Charles Stephenson, Port Hope; A.J. Runnals, Hope Township; T.A. Reid, Clarke Township; John Smith, Cavan Township; Edward Youngman, Manvers Township.

Also, about this time, two committees were appointed: a rural committee composed of fourteen men prominent in rural matters from different parts of Southern Ontario; and a natural resources research committee composed of thirteen men especially interested in conservation, some of whom had been members of the Guelph Conference in 1941.

By the fall of 1944, although there seemed to be ample proof that a new approach to conservation in Southern Ontario should be made, the minister decided that it would be helpful to bring together all those interested in such work for further affirmation of the need. Accordingly, the natural resources research committee met in Mr Porter's office to plan such a conference, the theme of which would be 'River Valley Development in Southern Ontario.'

The author attended as a representative of the Department of Lands and Forests; a conference was planned provided he could be seconded to the new Department of Planning and Development. This transfer was subsequently arranged. Mr Porter then asked Dr J.D. Detwiler, professor of applied biology, University of Western Ontario, to chair a local committee to assist in planning the conference, which was proposed for London, Ontario.

The London conference was held 13–14 October 1944. Its purpose was to provide an opportunity for groups and individuals in Southern Ontario who had been grappling with the conservation problem to discuss the various types of work which should be done. Invitations to attend the conference were sent to all municipalities in the river valleys of Southern Ontario, educators, government officials, and executives of all organizations of the province interested in conservation. The registered attendance was 250, a representative cross-section of the citizens of Southern Ontario.

The conference delegates were welcomed by the Honourable Dana Porter and His Worship, Colonel W.G. Heaman, mayor of London. In his address of welcome, the minister sounded the keynote:

It is a very great pleasure indeed, as the head of this new Department of Planning and Development, to extend a welcome to you here today.

Ever since this department of the government was established last May, Dr Langford has been devoting a great deal of his time to the consideration of the sort of problems that we have come here to discuss.

If the problem of flood control, which exists not only in the Thames valley but in other river valleys of the province, is to be tackled in an effective way, it seems to us that a great many complicated factors will have to be taken into consideration.

We have come to the conclusion that there is no one simple solution of the problems that are before us. For that reason we thought it would serve a purpose to hold a meeting of this kind, consisting of the representatives of the municipalities in this river valley and the Grand River valley and in certain other places – we have here representatives from the Ganaraska valley, where the town of Port Hope is situated – for the purpose not only of hearing from men of experience in various lines of conservation, and in matters relating to flood control, but also that we may have a discussion from the delegates here as to their views on how this situation might be handled in a practical way.

Now, it seems to me that in view of the rather complicated nature of various problems that will be before us that we must not look for any quick and ready and simple solution of the problems, but we must try to regard it rather as one that will need a programme which may extend over the next ten years for its final completion. It will involve in some places a reforestation programme. In others it may have to do with the present system of drainage that exists in some parts of this country. It may have to do in some parts of the country with agricultural methods that are being followed. It may also result in certain public works being required. In no one of these various fields of enquiry can we find the whole solution.

We will hear later during this conference about the work that has already been done by way of a survey on the Ganaraska valley. We have decided that work should commence as soon as possible to carry out the recommendations of that survey and to formulate a policy which will be carried out in that much smaller valley than the Thames. There, to some extent, we may be able to experiment and demonstrate what policies will be successful and what might turn out not to be so successful.

The main necessity in a programme of this kind is that it must have, to be really effective, the fullest possible cooperation and the fullest understanding not only of the technical men who may be engaged in working it out, but on the part of the people who are living in the region. They will be most closely affected by the policies that are adopted, and that is one reason why a conference of this kind can be of great value. Unless we can, in the course of working out our policy, keep the public fully advised and fully aware of the nature of the problems and unless we can carry their continued support, any policy that may be attempted by any government will be sure to fail.

Therefore, I think that in view of the large response that has resulted from the invitations that have been issued to this conference, it is quite apparent that the public is fully aware that the problem exists and is determined that some solution, or a number of solutions perhaps, will be found and applied.

May I conclude by saying once again that we welcome you here on behalf of this department of the government, and we look forward to fruitful results from the meeting that is assembled here.

Dr G.B. Langford, director of the Department of Planning and Development acted as chairman for the first session at which the following papers were presented: 'The Need of River Valley Development in Ontario,' by Professor A.F. Coventry; 'The Story of the Muskingum Project,' by Bryce C. Browning; and 'The Need for

Urban and Rural Cooperation in River Valley Development,' by Watson H. Porter. At dinner, Dr W.A. Albreckt, soils department, College of Agriculture, University of Missouri, Columbia, Missouri, was the guest speaker. The first part of Dr Albreckt's address was broadcast over radio station CFPL. Following the address, a number of motion picture films were shown depicting water power, wildlife, modern methods of farm tillage, and other subjects describing the general field of conservation.

William Phillip, chairman of the Grand River Conservation Commission, Galt, acted as chairman for the Saturday morning meeting at which the following papers were presented: 'Reforestation as a Means of Controlling Run-off,' by E.J. Zavitz; 'Erosion Control and Soil Conservation,' by Professor G.N. Ruhnke; 'Underground Water Supplied,' by Dr J.F. Caley; and 'Stream Sanitation,' by Dr A.E. Berry. The Saturday noon luncheon was in charge of the Ontario Conservation and Reforestation Association with the president, Dr J.H. Munro, of Maxville, presiding. At this meeting, the Honourable W.G. Thompson, minister of the Department of Lands and Forests, officially released the Ganaraska report, after which J.D. Thomas presented the minister with a copy of the report, bound in leather. E.K. Hampson, chairman of the Guelph Conference, Hamilton, then gave a brief talk on the origin and significance of the Ganaraska report.

An interesting feature of the conference was an exhibition of maps, bulletins, books and about one hundred photographs kindly loaned by government departments, universities and delegates. These were studied carefully by those in attendance and helped to supplement the information which was presented by the various speakers.

The most instructive address was given by Bryce Browning, secretary-treasurer of the Muskingum Conservancy District, Ohio; many of the problems of the Muskingum district are the same or analagous to those in Southern Ontario. Mr Browning used as his text, 'Where there is no vision the people perish,' and it is interesting to recall how this verse from Proverbs has been appropriated and used down through the years by the Ontario authorities in their public relations literature.

Professor J.D. Detwiler, president of the Canadian Conservation Association, London, was chairman of the Saturday afternoon session. Two papers were presented at this meeting: 'Grand River Conservation,' by E.F. Roberts; and 'A Reconnaissance Survey of the Upper Thames Watershed,' by W.R. Smith. This was followed by a report and presentation of resolutions by Professor R.F. Leggett, chairman of the resolutions committee.

Our request, Mr Chairman, is that if the resolutions which we wish to present are accepted by the meeting, you would be good enough to pass them, Sir, to the Honourable Dana Porter, with the request that he present them from this conference to the premier of the province.

The first resolution is the most important and the most general, and before I read it I want to say one word of explanation. In seeking the setting up of a central authority, we are using the term 'conservation authority,' but the word 'authority' has a small 'a.' I do want to make that clear because we do not feel we should suggest the type of authority; it may be a modification of existing departments, it may be a commission, it may be some new body. All we do wish to suggest is that some central agency should be set up.

Therefore, Mr Chairman, as I read the resolution, would you please remember when I use the term 'conservation authority,' I am using it in the general sense, and not to designate any specific type of single agency.

Resolution No. 1:

WHEREAS there is urgent need for an active programme of conservation of renewable natural resources of Ontario – water, soil, crops, forests, fish and wildlife; and

WHEREAS all renewable natural resources must always be considered as parts of an integrated whole, and not individually, in all phases of conservation;

THEREFORE BE IT RESOLVED that the government of Ontario be urged to establish a conservation authority for Ontario, responsible to the government, having as its principal function the bringing about of coordination and co-operation amongst all agencies in Ontario carrying on and promoting conservation projects with the object of formulating and putting into effect a unified programme for the rehabilitation and wise use of all our renewable natural resources.

Amongst the specific steps which should be taken by such an authority are:

a/Assisting in the promotion of local conservancy projects throughout the province;

b/Acquiring, by purchase or otherwise, submarginal areas to be held in trust for conservancy purposes;

c/Ensuring that all works intended for flood control purposes are properly correlated with the general principles of conservation practice;

d/Considering the operations of the existing drainage acts in relation to conservancy work with a view to the prevention of the use of these acts for the drainage of lands which should preferably be left undrained;

e/Maintaining contact with neighbouring provinces and states for the assembly and exchange of information and the correlation of appropriate programmes of work in relation to natural resources common to Ontario and neighbouring areas;

f/Assisting in the training of technical personnel for the carrying out of conservational work; and

g/Fostering the direction of adequate attention to all phases of the conservation of natural resources in all the educational work of the province of Ontario.

Resolution No. 2:

WHEREAS the wellbeing of all renewable natural resources is fundamentally dependent upon adequate ground-water supplies; and

WHEREAS it is believed that the ground-water levels in southern Ontario are generally receding;

THEREFORE BE IT RESOLVED that the government of Ontario be urged to arrange for an early start and an inventory of ground-water supplies in Ontario, in conjunction with the Geological Survey of Canada.

At the final meeting of the London conference the Honourable Dana Porter said:

When this meeting was first conceived I don't think that any of us pictured the great success with which it has met during the last two days. It is very gratifying indeed to us of the Department of Planning and Development – and I am sure to the government as a whole – to find the very wide-spread interest that has been shown in the problems that have been before us.

I may say it is also very gratifying to find that in other parts of the province, as a result of the success of this meeting, a similar meeting is desired, and I hope that in due time we may give full consideration to the resolution directed to that end.

I would like to say that the success of this meeting is really due to the activities of certain voluntary associations which have been going on for the last – well, I don't know how many years. Sometimes it is necessary, in order to bring an idea to fruition to be prepared to spend perhaps ten years of development before full recognition may be obtained. Nevertheless, we seem to have arrived at the point where we can expect full and even enthusiastic public support to a really forward-looking policy of conservation, and I may say that we have reached this point as the result of a great deal of work that has been done over the past number of years by groups of men who have interested themselves and devoted themselves to work of this kind.

If the minister and Dr Langford had had some doubts before the conference of the enthusiasm for a Conservation Branch in the department, these must have been pleasantly brushed aside by the enthusiasm of the delegates.

Following the evening meeting on Saturday 14 October, with the minister and Dr Langford in attendance, the formation of a conservation branch was discussed and Mr Richardson was asked to transfer from lands and forests to head the new branch with the title of chief conservation engineer. That transfer was arranged on 1 November 1944.

In order to get 'in the mood' and to observe the techniques of a successfully managed conservation programme, it was decided that a task force should spend a week on the Muskingum reserve in mid-November. As the Ganaraska advisory board had been appointed in August, it was decided to take some of the leaders from that area and one from the upper Thames valley as well. The party included Fred Bowen, chairman of the Ganaraska advisory board; A.S. Miller, county engineer for the United Counties of Northumberland and Durham; Edward Summers, agricultural representative for Durham County; and W. Raywood (Jim) Smith, county engineer for Middlesex County. Bryce Browning and his staff in Ohio spared neither time nor expense in explaining all phases of their work, and this, together with their lavish hospitality, made the trip exceedingly fruitful.

It soon became obvious that the Conservation Authorities Branch was pioneering in new fields. There were no terms of reference, no guide lines to follow, and until a conservation authorities act was produced to present to the municipalities, the branch was really not in business.

It was soon found there is something exhilarating about working in a new small department. The branch heads had access at all times to the minister and the director and the whole staff worked together as one big family. It is also interesting to record, especially during these present days of burgeoning budgets, that the amount in the estimates for the whole department for the first year was $100,000. There were no strings attached, no treasury board to worry about; the minister had a free hand. However, it is recalled that some wondered how it would be possible to spend that much money in one year. In 1961 the budget of the branch alone was about $2.25 million and by 1970 it had risen to $16.143 million, most of which was in the form of grants to the thirty-eight authorities.

In 1944, office space in Toronto was at a premium. The small staff – except for the minister and director of the department – was located in a large old dwelling – 15 Queen's Park Crescent. Within the house the only place available was a former butler's pantry, approximately ten by eighteen feet at the rear of the dining room. Here, in these minimal quarters, the Conservation Branch set up business.

The first task was the preparation of a bill for the legislature which, if passed, would become the Conservation Authorities Act. Certain sections of the Grand River Conservation Commission Act which had little to do with the broad field of conservation, but which contained many legal safeguards for the type of work which the commission – and, in this case, the authority – must do, were incorporated in the bill, but new material covering the new approach to conservation had to be added. Accordingly, a few guide lines were prepared which would be *sine quo non* as far as the new bill was concerned:

1/An authority shall be formed only by the petition of the municipalities in a watershed; in other words the people must initiate the authority.

2/An authority shall be a body corporate thus assuring that the autonomy of the authority will be inviolate.

3/An authority shall initiate its own schemes concerning flood control, land use, forestry, wildlife and other matters within the framework of the Conservation Authorities Act.

4/An authority shall have power to expropriate land.

5/An authority shall elect its own officers, hire its own staff, engage consulting engineers and other specialists.

6/An authority shall cooperate with and receive assistance from other departments of the government.

7/An authority shall obtain its funds from taxes raised by the member municipalities and solicit grants from the two senior governments.

Bill 81 was ready for the 1945 session of the legislature. However, when the session was well under way, an altercation developed between the government and the opposition, the Co-operative Commonwealth Federation (CCF), with the result that the premier dissolved the legislature. This meant that a large number of bills were left over to the following year – one of which was Bill 81.

The dissolution of the legislature and the postponement of the conservation authorities act provided a welcome hiatus for completing the new branch's plans. It was evident that as each authority became established it would have to be given some clear-cut guidance, as the members could not be expected to search out conservation problems in their watersheds, some of which were extensive, and carry them through to completion. It seemed reasonable therefore, and was so decided, that as each authority came into being, a conservation survey of the watershed would be made, following much the same pattern as the Ganaraska survey; the report of each survey would then serve as a working plan for years to come. To do this, it was necessary to engage a small technical staff in the Conservation Branch to head the different sections of work to be included in the survey, under whom the required number of students from the universities would be engaged to serve as field men during the summer months.

The original technical staff was: A.H. Richardson, MA, SM silv, FE, P ENG, chief conservation engineer; A.S.L. Barnes, BSCF, RPF, forestry; C.E. Bush, BASC, OLS, P ENG, engineering; Leslie Laking, BSA, Kew graduate, land use; Verschoyle B. Blake, history; H.J. Christian, accountant; and Professor G. Ross Lord, SM, PH D, P ENG, University of Toronto, consultant in hydraulic engineering.

The following were added later: J.W. Murray, BA SC, P Eng, hydraulic engineering; K.M. Mayall, MA, BSC F, wildlife and recreation; H.F. Crown, BSA, extension; and Professor F.D. Ide, MA, PH D, University of Toronto, consultant in fish culture.

Following the London conference, the citizens of London and the municipalities on the upper Thames commenced to bestir themselves about flood-control problems, problems which had been set aside because of the war. A steering committee with editor Watson Porter as chairman was appointed, and requested the minister to make a conservation survey of the upper Thames. Although policy had established that a survey would not be carried out until an authority was established, in view of the fact that the passage of the act had been postponed for a year, the minister decided to proceed with the upper Thames survey in 1945. However, it was clearly pointed out that although the control of flooding was uppermost in the minds of most people in the area, the survey would not be confined to this one problem, but would investigate the complementary problems of land use, forestry, wildlife and recreation and that action would be expected on these as well as flood control, if an authority were established.

In looking through the Thames report of 1945 it is interesting to note some of the problems which were dealt with which are absent from later reports. For example, there is an eleven-page discussion on the general topic of ground water, a survey of the farm water supply of the Trout Creek watershed and a portion of the middle branch in which 287 reports were obtained from 95 percent of occupied farms in the Trout Creek area; a full discussion of the city of London water supply, including a proposal that a pipeline be built either from Lake Erie (at a cost of $5 million) or Lake Huron ($7 million); a discussion on sources of pollution in the river under agricultural drainage; industrial waste, and domestic waste; and lastly a strong warning against the folly of allowing encroachments on the natural flood plain of the river by any actions of man.

The report was presented to the upper Thames steering committee at a large gathering of interested citizens, in the Hotel London in October 1946 by the Honourable Dana Porter. It was given wide coverage throughout the province by the press and evoked an interesting cartoon in the Toronto *Daily Star* by Les Callan, the staff cartoonist, who sent me the original drawing as a souvenir of the occasion.

Also during the summer of 1945, in response to a resolution passed at the London conference, a ground-water survey was carried out in Southern Ontario for the Conservation Branch by Professor C.S. Gwynne, associate professor of geology, Iowa State College, Ames, Iowa, assisted by Archie K. Watt, BA. The report runs to eighty-seven typewritten pages.

The purpose of this preliminary survey [Professor Gwynne wrote] was to find out what is known regarding ground-water resources of the area and of the geology which bears upon it and to determine the areas of communities having ground-water problems, to whom assistance might be given by a government service to be established for the purpose and to recommend a future course of ground-water survey.

Methods employed in the survey included research in all literature dealing with the regional geology, a visit to each of forty-one counties in Southern Ontario, and conferences with agencies and individuals to gather information bearing on the geology of ground-water and problems which had arisen in connection with these. The agencies and individuals visited included senior government departments, public utility commissions, well-drilling companies, agricultural representatives, county, city and consulting engineers, mayors, and reeves. Individuals consulted during the survey numbered 152.

The report contained nine recommendations, the most important of which is, 'The need for the establishment of a permanent organization devoted to ground-water work in Southern Ontario.'

It was thought at the time that Professor Gwynne's most important recommendation would be implemented by the appointment of a geologist to the staff of the Conservation Branch, but as ground-water studies are intimately related to Pleistocene geology the ground-water organization was assigned to the Department of Mines with Archie Watt in charge. Subsequently, in 1957 when the Ontario Water Resources Commission was established, this branch was transferred to the commission.

The Conservation Authorities Act was passed during the 1946 session of the legislature, after which the reaction from the municipalities was awaited. The first authorities formed were the Etobicoke and the Ausable on 30 July. These two regions had pressing flood-control problems and areas suitable for extensive reforestation. These and several others, comprising watersheds whose people had a lively awareness of the need of conservation in their areas, formed an authority at the first statutory meeting. Twelve others, however, were apprehensive about the need of such a programme and of these, six required two such meetings, two required three, three required four and one required five.

Ten authorities were established in the first three years, which put quite a burden on the small technical staff. After that the number each year thinned out somewhat, although in two of the succeeding years four authorities were formed.

From the foregoing it might seem that there was a continuous flow of new authorities being formed each year; this however was not the case, as there were also a few lean years.

3
... and the Heavens Opened

Flooding is a natural phenomenon. As long as rain has fallen there have been floods, and in recent years it seems they are becoming more frequent, more violent, and more destructive.

Floods are associated with the spring break-up and this is the time of the year when they often do most damage, but in Ontario the record shows that serious floods have occurred in every month of the year.

The earliest reference to flooding is found in Ziesburger's diary of 1792 when the site of the Moravian village of Fairfield – a few miles downstream from London – was being chosen. The diary states that the Thames River rose 20 feet. Mention is also made of a flood which occurred in 1813 in the village of Port Hope on the Ganaraska River which carried away the bridge on the main street. On 13 September 1878 flooding was so severe in certain parts of Ontario that ballotting in the federal election was postponed. Today, flooding of such severity would provoke immediate government response; in earlier times, though, floods were little more than another hardship to be borne and forgotten.

Ontario was settled where her rivers flow. As population increased the permanent structures of a growing citizenry encroached more and more on the rivers' flood plains. When flood waters rolled over river banks, homes, barns, municipal buildings were swept from their foundations. In this sense – the obliteration or damage of man-made structures – the damage from floods increased as civilization extended. It is safe to assume that no river of any size in Southern Ontario did not exact its toll on the settlers along its banks.

The Humber River is but one example. Records from the earliest years of settlement to 1954 – the year of Hurricane Hazel – reveal that the Humber has burst its bounds on seventy-eight occasions. Of these, twenty-five are classed as severe, one as very severe.

Two of the largest rivers in Ontario, the Grand and the Thames, suffered periodically from this scourge, so it is not surprising that the residents who inhabited their shores were the first to plan for adequate control. Over the years

Brampton, Main Street on 16 March 1948. Like many Ontario cities situated in a
river valley, Brampton had become resigned to its river (the Etobicoke)
overflowing its banks on a more-or-less regular schedule.

prominent citizens along the course of the Grand had agitated for some means of
control, and after the destructive flood of 1912 the voices for remedial measures
became more strident. Leadership was given by a group of civil engineers in the
valley, whose agitation led to the formation in 1931 of the Grand River Valley
Boards of Trade, an organization representing the municipalities which had suffered most. The boards approached the Ontario government requesting that a
survey and report be made to establish ways and means of controlling floods and
improving summer flow.

Through the minister of lands and forests, arrangements were made with the
chairman of the Ontario Hydro Electric Power Commission of Ontario, who assigned James McIntosh of the hydraulic staff to prepare a report on the Grand River
drainage and make recommendations for the necessary controls. The survey was
carried out as requested and the report was transmitted to the minister on 11
February 1932. The McIntosh report indicated that control of floods and the
conservation of water for summer flow were feasible. Representation was then
made to the Ontario government for legislation which would permit the
municipalities to proceed with the work.

The first reponse from the government was the passing of the Grand River

Galt, Water Street in early spring 1928. After spring break-up, the flood-swollen waters of the Grand River swept over its banks and left behind giant ice cubes to block the city's streets.

Conservation Commission Act in 1932. Little action was taken and, when the Grand River Conservation Commission Act of 1938 was passed, the first act was repealed.

In the act of 1938, eight municipalities were named: the cities of Brantford, Galt and Kitchener, the towns of Paris, Preston and Waterloo and the villages of Elora and Fergus. The specific work which the commission was authorized to do is summarized in Section 8 of the act:

a/ to study and investigate, itself or its engineers or other employees or representatives, the Grand River valley, and to determine a scheme whereby the waters of the said Grand River valley may be conserved to afford a sufficient supply of water for the municipal, domestic and manufacturing purposes of the participating municipalities during periods of water shortages and controlled in times of flood, and to undertake such schemes.

b/ to erect works and create reservoirs by the construction of dams or otherwise.

The first structures planned were the Shand Dam on the main river, two miles upstream from Fergus, with a storage capacity of 46,000 acre-feet, and the Luther Marsh Dam. The estimated cost of these two dams at that time was approximately $2 million. This amount was considered too great for the eight municipalities to finance on their own; consequently, the commission requested the government of Canada to contribute 37.5 percent, the Ontario government 37.5 percent, the remaining 25 percent to be paid by the benefiting municipalities on a pro rated basis to be decided by the commission and adjusted to the benefit to be received.

It is not clear why the commission settled on 25 percent as the municipalities'

Port Hope, at the mouth of the Ganaraska River, was periodically inundated by the river in flood. The railway bridge remained intact – though its piers may have suffered – but the approaches to the vehicular and pedestrian bridge in the background were awash.

share, but it would seem that this percentage was deemed the maximum that the municipalities could raise. The senior governments agreed as requested, and so, at this time, the familiar formula of 37.5–37.5–25 percent, which has been used over the years for sharing the cost of large flood control schemes, was established.

In 1939 the commission commenced work on the Shand Dam and completed it in August 1942. Because Canada was at war it was decided to delay the building of the Luther Marsh Dam.

For many years the municipalities on the Thames River had been plagued with floods. In 1937, in late April, the valley suffered a severe flood which, if not the largest in its history, was certainly the most destructive. All sections of the valley were affected, the greatest damage being suffered in the city of London.

As on the Grand, the people in the Thames valley had been agitating for years for some means of control, but following the flood of 1937, a concerted approach by the larger municipalities was made to the Ontario government. Again, through the Ontario Hydro Electric Power Commission, a hydraulic survey was made and this report, 'Thames River Preliminary Report on Flood Control,' was transmitted to the government on 27 April 1938. Subsequently Government control measures were set forth in the Act to Provide for Control of Waters in the Thames River, 1943, and the act named as participating municipalities, the cities of London, Woodstock, Stratford and Chatham, and the towns of Ingersoll, St Marys, and Mitchell. The act also provided for the appointment of a commission to be known as the Thames River Control Commission.

In intent and purpose the Thames River control act of 1943 is the same as the Grand River Conservation Commission Act of 1938. However, in 1943, with Canada at war, it was necessary to defer the implementation of the act. In 1944, the

One of the first dams built in Ontario was the Shand Dam of 1942 on the notoriously unpredictable Grand. The dam was built by the Grand River Conservation Commission, the predecessor of the present authority.

Department of Planning and Development including the Conservation Branch was established and preparation of the Conservation Authorities Act was under way. Consequently, when this latter act was passed in 1946, the Thames River control act was not required.

On 15 and 16 October 1954, Hurricane Hazel passed through Ontario.

Hurricane Hazel travelled north from Haiti [the meterorological office reported] hitting the north shore of Lake Ontario at 11:10 PM on Friday, 15 October. The eye of the storm, carrying with it heavy, warm tropical air, met a cold front travelling eastward across Canada which resulted in abnormal rainfall.

The hurricane passed directly over Toronto, proceeded north, passing over North Bay at 1:30 the next morning and from there it headed into the south end of James Bay dissipating itself in these unrecorded areas.

This resultant abnormal rain together with abnormally high winds was experienced roughly over an area starting at Chatham on the west, northward to Blind River then eastward through North Bay to Mattawa, then south to Port Hope. The evidence of some of the public utilities shows that the wind storm also branched off in a northeasterly direction up the Ottawa valley almost into the city of Ottawa.

The greatest concentration of rainfall was around Brampton where eight inches was recorded in forty-eight hours and the greatest damage occurred at the mouths of the streams emptying into Lake Ontario in the vicinity of Toronto, notably the Humber River and the Etobicoke Creek.

Hazel did much damage in other parts of the province as well as in Metropolitan Toronto region but it was here, because of the concentration of two million people

Woodbridge, Clarence Street during the disastrous Hurricane Hazel of October 1954.

and the six small rivers which drain an area of 1,000 square miles, that so much damage was done. Another important factor was that the autumn of 1954 was unusually wet, with the result that when Hurricane Hazel struck, the watersheds had already reached their absorptive capacity.

Following Hurricane Hazel, the government of Canada appointed a Commission on Hurricane Damage in Ontario and the government of Ontario established the Flood Homes and Building Assistance Board of Ontario. The terms of reference for the commission on hurricane damage are contained in the Order-in-Council, PC No. 1610, 20 October 1954 and read:

That Messrs John B. Carswell [formerly chairman of the Fraser Valley Dyking Board] and D. Bruce Shaw of the city of Toronto, in the province of Ontario, be appointed commissioners under the Inquiries Act to inquire into the nature and extent of the damage caused by the flood in and adjoining the Humber River valley in Ontario, the cost of fighting the flood, and the providing of emergency relief required because of the flood, and of the precautions to be taken to guard against the recurrence of such flood conditions, in order to make available at the earliest possible date a complete statement of all the essential facts necessary to determine what provisions should be made by the governments in respect of the said flood.

The report consists of seventeen pages, and since these are stamped confidential it is not permissible to comment on the findings or recommendations. However, it is permissible to repeat the information given to the commissioners and to relate their reaction to the plans which were outlined. The conservation programme which each conservation authority could carry out was described under the five headings which are so familiar today: water, land use, forestry, wildlife and recreation. It was also stated that the Humber authority was planning a number of dams and other structures to control flooding, improve summer flow and make extensive use of flood plain lands for recreation.

The commissioners agreed with the desirability of using the flood plain lands for recreation but gave no encouragement for the building of dams or hydraulic structures of any kind. On the contrary, they stated that in their opinion the whole valley should be cleared of as many structures as possible; when the flood waters came, give them a clear path and stand aside. When they gave this solution for handling the flood waters of the Humber, it was realized that these two amiable gentlemen were living in the past and were unfamiliar with the new philosophy of conservation. Such a solution was vigorously opposed and the commission was assured that the Humber authority – and any other authority in the province – would not follow such old-fashioned advice. Furthermore, it was pointed out that such a plan would turn the Humber River into a gigantic storm sewer, wreaking havoc by erosion and, in summer, creating a sluggish, polluted stream which would be totally incompatible with a well-planned recreation area.

The damage done by Hurricane Hazel can be grouped in the following categories: public properties – roads, culverts, bridges; public utilities – electricity, telephone, railways, water, sewers; commercial and industrial properties; houses and contents, house trailers; agriculture; parklands; flood fighting and clearing; and emergency relief. Various estimates have been made of the dollar damage wrought by Hurricane Hazel: the most satisfactory figure is $20 million. The one value which can never be calculated is the loss of eighty-one lives, mostly by drowning.

The Flood Homes and Building Assistance Board was created 4 November 1954 with the following members: Norman W. Long, chairman; John T. Bryden; John S. Entwistle; and Ross Booth, secretary. The terms of reference for the board are covered in orders-in-council, November 1954 and February 1955, and the pertinent sections for the purpose of this history are: 'The board shall investigate and appraise the damage to or destruction of privately owned dwellings, barns, storages, workshops and other buildings caused by the flood waters from the main river and tributaries of the Humber and other affected areas in the province on 15 and 16 October 1954.

'Upon the basis of the appraised damage to or destruction of such buildings, the board may make assistance payments to the owner.'

The maximum amount paid on account of structural damage in any one case was $5,000 and this was shared half and half by the federal and provincial governments.

An order-in-council made provision also for the purchase of land on which buildings had been destroyed and adjacent land which was subject to flooding. 'The board may, as an agent for the province of Ontario, make payments to the municipalities to assist them in the acquisition of lands and premises in flood areas upon such terms and for such prices as may be directed by the attorney-general for Ontario.'

The implementation of the above paragraphs was covered by two agreements, one for the municipalities outside of Metropolitan Toronto and the other for Metro. The agreement for the municipalities outside of Metro provided that when lands are acquired they shall be held by the municipality for and on behalf of the province and shall be used and disposed of as the government may direct. Also that 'no structures, buildings or works shall be built or erected upon the said lands and premises' without the consent of the government. The agreement with Metropolitan Toronto was similar except that 'lands' shall be held by Metro and never in the future be used for residential, commercial or industrial purposes. In most cases the lands were eventually deeded to the appropriate conservation authorities.

The board completed the bulk of its work in the fall of 1955 and submitted its report to the Honourable Leslie M. Frost, premier of Ontario, 7 November 1955 at which time the board was dissolved. The few accounts outstanding were transferred to the Conservation Branch for completion and when these had been paid the amount expended was:

Assistance programmes	$ 727,367
Property purchases	1,793,499
Total	$2,520,866

Generally, the province paid the full cost of property acquisition (flood-plain lands) in the municipalities outside of Metro, and 75 percent of the cost within Metro; the major exception was the village of Long Branch for which the province paid Metro 50 percent. The federal government did not participate in the purchase of flood-plain lands.

In her wake Hazel left debris, disaster and death. But when she had passed and when the initial shock had been assimilated, the horror that had been Hazel brought important advances in conservation. The most important was the public recognition that flood control and water conservation are but two sides of the same coin; a river system must be dealt with as a single unit, with a coordinated plan put into effect over a number of years. The philosophy was not new – the reports of most conservation authorities for a number of years had emphasized this very point. It had been difficult to persuade the public that new and potentially more disastrous floods were the promise of the future unless control measures were implemented; and governments of any level seldom act unless their constituents are aroused. Hazel was a powerful arouser.

After Hurricane Hazel, three river systems in the province which were sorely in need of control – the upper Thames, the Ausable and the rivers of the Metropolitan Toronto region – launched corrective programmes.

The Upper Thames River Conservation Authority submitted a brief on flood control and water conservation to the governments of Canada and Ontario. The brief called for a ten-year plan which would include the construction of five dams, river-bed channel improvements at three locations and a total cost estimated to be $9.641 million. The cost was to be shared, the brief suggested, on the now familiar

37.5 – 37.5 – 25 percent formula. The two governments approved the plan and two agreements were signed on 28 January 1961, one between the government of Canada and the government of Ontario, the second between Ontario and the authority. Construction work was started soon after.

The Metropolitan Toronto and Region Conservation Authority also submitted a brief on flood control and water conservation which set forth a plan including the building of fifteen dams and improvement works on three rivers at a cost of $38.9 million to be constructed over ten years. To finance this scheme the Canadian government insisted that for ten of the proposed dams and river improvement projects, to cost a total of $24 million, the federal government carry 37.5 percent, the provincial government a like percentage, and the local authority carry 25 percent. For five smaller dams to cost $2.6 million, it was stipulated the province and authority split the cost evenly. Similarly, for the purchase of flood-plain lands it was specified the province and authority each pay half the estimated $12.3 million. The governments agreed to the plan and agreements were signed on 14 June 1961.

The Ausable River Conservation Authority submitted a brief for the construction of the Parkhill Dam at an estimated cost of $826,000. The governments approved the plan and the agreements were signed on 28 January 1961.

In addition to the grants the government of Canada requested that the three authorities submit for approval a cost-benefit study of the projects and a programme for ancillary conservation measures including reforestation, construction of recreational areas and overnight campsites.

The second advance in conservation attributable to Hurricane Hazel was the acknowledgement by the government of Ontario that the acquisition of flood-plain lands was an integral part of a flood control project. The first sign of this acknowledgement was evident when the Flood Homes and Buildings Assistance Board purchased the flood-plain lands on which many damaged homes were situated and transferred the ownership of the land to the municipalities and subsequently to the conservation authorities. Later, when the agreement was negotiated between the two senior governments and the Metropolitan Toronto and Region Conservation Authority for the ten-year flood-control plan, the federal government decided not to share in the cost of flood-plain lands. Immediately, Premier Leslie M. Frost of Ontario came to the rescue of the authority and agreed that the cost of these lands would be shared evenly by Ontario and the authority. By this decision of the premier the new policy for the acquisition of flood plain lands throughout Ontario was confirmed. (Over the years conservationists have maintained that *all* river flood plains – and, in some cases, the whole river valley – should be reserved; many flood plains are now being developed as public parks. These matters will be detailed later in the section on recreation.)

The third advance that Hazel spurred was the appointing of a hydrometeorologist to the Conservation Branch. Climate is obviously the major factor determining a region's water resources. After all, the source of all fresh water on earth is precipitation and the major water losses from the earth's surface occur through evaporation to the atmosphere. However, it is much less obvious how knowledge of the weather can be used to solve practical problems in water resources development and flood control. The specialized field of applied meteorology which deals with this subject is known as hydrometeorology.

Too often, a disaster must occur before the need of scientific research and activity in a particular field can be brought home to the public. The loss of life and the tremendous flood damage caused by Hurricane Hazel in October 1954, produced the first concerted and continuing efforts in hydrometeorology to be undertaken in Canada.

In 1948 Dr Andrew Thomson chief of the head office of the Meteorological Branch in Toronto invited Merril Bernard, chief of the climatological and hydrologic division of the US Weather Bureau to give a series of lectures on the subject of hydrometeorology. Clayton Bush and John Murray, who constituted the hydraulic section of the Conservation Branch, attended the lectures and brought back the proposal that it would be a useful addition to the staff if we could engage the services of a hydrometeorologist. At that time, when only a few authorities had been formed, it was agreed that it was premature to apply for such an appointment but six years later, after Hurricane Hazel, the time was definitely opportune. After receiving approval from the Honourable W.K. Warrender, minister of the department, the problem was taken to Dr Thomson. He was enthusiastic about the proposal and recommended to his superiors that such an appointment be made. On 1 February 1955 the Honourable George Marler, minister of transport, Ottawa, wrote to the Honourable W.K. Warrender that the DOT would be prepared to assign a meteorologist for this work for a period of six months; the government of Canada would pay the meteorologist's salary for that period and the Ontario government would supply office space and any other expenses incidental to carrying out the work. This arrangement was agreed to and J.P. Bruce, MA, was assigned to the Conservation Branch in October 1955.

At the end of the trial period it was agreed that the same arrangements would be continued for an indefinite period with review by both federal and provincial departments to insure that the position met the requirements as they were initially established. In October 1958 Mr Bruce was transferred to other duties and D.N. McMullen was appointed to fill the position. Secondment of a hydrometeorologist to the Conservation Branch ended in December 1969. At that time Mr McMullen was appointed hydrometeorologist with the Conservation Branch.

To give the reader a summary of the important work done by this section a few excerpts will be included from a paper entitled 'An Integrated System of Flood Forecasting and River Control in the Province of Ontario, Canada,' by D.N. McMullen read at the International Conference on Water for Peace, 23 to 31 May 1967 at Washington, DC.

Dam design and reservoir operation
The conservation authorities have been involved in a broad-scale dam construction programme for many years with the engineering division of the branch having the responsibility for the design, construction and control of these dams.

An important feature of this programme is that all the reservoirs are developed on the basis of multi-purpose use of water. These uses, which include flood control, urban water supply, irrigation, pollution abatement, maintenance of flow and recreation are often incompatible and as a consequence create many operational problems not encountered in the single-purpose reservoir.

A flood-control reservoir requires empty storage space for flood waters; a water-supply reservoir should be full at the beginning of the season with drawdown taking place through the season; a recreation reservoir requires a constant level throughout the summer season. To coordinate such uses within one reservoir requires that flood-routing techniques and reservoir operation procedures be thoroughly established at the design stage to ensure that the hydraulic characteristics of the structure effectively meet these procedures.

It is also of importance that reservoir-operation procedures be established within the realistic capabilities of the flood-forecast service. Without this consideration the efficiency of the reservoir for its various uses is decreased markedly, or alternatively, the safety of the structure is imperilled.

As an example of these requirements consider a multi-purpose reservoir for flood control, water supply and recreation which has only limited storage capacity in relation to the potential flood runoff from the basin. Starting with an empty reservoir at the beginning of the spring runoff, the pattern of discharge must be established on the basis of the forecast runoff pattern in order to reduce the peak flows as much as possible. These high flows from snowmelt usually cover a protracted period so that only limited reduction is possible. The use of the reservoir storage at this time must also be apportioned on the premise of rainstorms occurring in conjunction with the snowmelt runoff. After the release of excess water from flood storage, the water level in the reservoir is set at the holding level for water supply and recreation. Procedures based on the gradual drawdown of water, within the limitations imposed by recreation, then come into operation. As autumn in Ontario has a high flood potential, reservoir drawdown must continue on schedule to insure the availability of flood storage space at the end of summer. At all stages in the reservoir programme, operations are more efficient when closely tied to river forecasts.

It is worthy of note, that in a multi-purpose reservoir system the releasing of stored water before a storm, to gain additional flood-control storage without compromising the other water uses, is an extremely difficult decision which can only be made on the advice of a dependable forecast service.

A thorough examination, during the design stage of the dam, of the hydrometeorological factors of the watershed as they affect the multi-uses of the reservoir, has proven to be a valuable means of improving the effectiveness of the operations. By such a study, control works can be designed to support the operation requirements.

To ensure this effectiveness of operation and the safety of the structure, a manual of operational procedures is established for each dam. In this way all persons connected with the operation of the dam are made fully aware of the procedures. The operating procedures include 'rule curves' which define release rates dependent on the rate of rise of the water level in the reservoir; water-holding levels for recreation and other uses; and water-release programmes for water supply and downstream pollution abatement.

These procedures are established by the engineering division of the branch in line with the water management policies established by the local conservation authority.

The actual operation of the dams is directed from regional control offices, handling one or

A stream gauge erected in 1960 by the Metropolitan Toronto and Region Conservation Authority. Similar gauges had been erected in the previous twenty years by the various authorities and the Grand commission.

more watersheds, which are under the direct control of the branch's central flood forecast and river control unit.

Flood forecasting

The first step in the warning programme is the issuance, in anticipation of a flood, of a flood advisory by the flood forecast and river control unit to the regional control offices. This insures that all operating staff are alerted to the emergency. The regional offices advise the dam operators as well as alerting the works department of the towns and cities within their region. These works departments are responsible for taking protective action along the rivers and streams as required.

When the full potential of the flood becomes evident, hydrographs are prepared for all affected streams and rivers based on anticipated snowmelt runoff or rainfall. These hydrographs are routed through the flood-control reservoirs on the basis of the designated operation procedures. The regional offices are then supplied with the routed forecast hydrograph and given advice on any supplementary operation procedures by which more effective use can be made of the available storage in the reservoir. The operation procedures for the full flood period are then reviewed by the regional office with the dam operators to make certain that all operations are known and clearly understood.

Flood forecasts are then issued to the public by press, radio and television giving information on the expected flood stage and the time and period of flooding at major locations along the rivers.

During the flood, the flood forecast and river control unit maintains a close watch on all meteorological information and streamflow data, adjusting forecasts and operation procedures as required to fit unforeseen developments. It is a basic understanding, however, that in the event of a major breakdown of communications, the operator of the dam follows the operation procedures laid down in his manual until communications are restored. This procedure ensures safety of the structure under all conditions while at the same time giving some reduction to flood flows.

A necessary complement for the proper functioning of a hydrometeorological section is the establishing of stream gauges on all rivers which are subject to flooding. This important matter was taken care of as soon as the conservation branch was established in 1944 with the result that since then the number of gauges installed as of 1 April 1970 is 138, of which 126 are automatic and only 12 are manually operated.

FLOOD CONTROL AGREEMENTS

In order to understand the difficulties which the authorities encountered in financing flood-control projects in the 1960s it is essential to establish a time sequence; the first period of time was that preceding the passing of the Canada Water Conservation Assistance Act on 14 May 1953, the second period was that which followed the act.

Up to this time four dams were built by the Grand commission and the authorities as individual projects. These were the Shand Dam, 1941; the Luther Marsh Dam, 1952; the Fanshawe Dam, 1953; and the Conestoga Dam, completed in 1958. Following the passing of the act, the federal government required that each authority prepare an overall flood-control plan embodying its proposals for dam construction and channel improvement. It also required that the authority concerned undertake certain ancillary measures in the fields of reforestation and recreation.

Though no standard procedures had been laid down, procedures had developed over the years which were recognized by all parties and which were followed religiously by the conservation authorities and the government of Ontario. When the commission or an authority proposed to build a dam and agreements had been signed, the authority prepared a plan indicating the location of the dam and reservoir and the lands which it proposed to purchase including lands which lay outside the area to be flooded. In nearly all cases these lands outside the reservoirs were parts of farms which had to be purchased in total because the owners were unwilling to sell a portion. This plan was approved in principle by the director of the branch and copies were forwarded to Ottawa. As individual properties came up for purchase they were inspected in the field by engineers of the branch. The engineers recommended the purchase of the property or declared it to be non-essential to the project or recommended the purchase of the whole property on condition that the authority sell valuable table land at a future date. The director of the branch then approved the engineer's recommendations and Ottawa was notified immediately.

To 1966 Ottawa had always accepted Ontario's approval of land purchases and had paid its agreed share of the cost, 37.5 percent, for land purchases. On 26 October 1966 the province received a letter signed by the Honourable Jean Luc Pépin, then minister of the Department of Northern Affairs and Natural Resources, stating that the federal government was not prepared to contribute its 37.5 percent grant to the purchase of lands above the high water mark of the reservoirs and that it would make this stipulation retroactive to the time the flood-control agreements were signed in 1961. It later demanded return of its grant on all land above the level of the top of the dam. The Wildwood Dam on the Thames and the Claireville Dam on the Humber had already been constructed and the Gordon Pittock Dam at Woodstock was nearing completion; lands for a number of other reservoirs had already been purchased and this created almost insuperable difficulties in financing for the province, the two authorities and their member municipalities. To the end of 1970 these problems had not been resolved.

Following passage of the Canada Water Conservation Assistance Act in 1953, a number of authorities prepared flood-control plans which were submitted to and approved by Ontario and then forwarded to Ottawa. These included the Upper Thames, the MTRCA, the Ausable, the Halton Region, the Moira, the Grand and the Credit authorities. The plans of the first four were approved in Ottawa but the last three were not.

The Ausable authority ran into difficulties of financing the Parkhill Dam when the Ontario Municipal Board limited the amount of money which the member municipalities (largely rural) could contribute towards the construction. After long negotiations the authority was able to get this project approved under the federal ARDA programme and for the only time in history an authority received grants from both governments covering approximately 90 percent of the cost.

The Halton region's plan was not really an overall flood control plan but the authority was fortunate that the federal government paid 37.5 percent of the first stage of its channel-improvement project. The federal government would not support the second stage of Halton's program.

The Credit authority, which is composed of rural municipalities in its upper reaches, was able later to get the Orangeville reservoir approved under the federal ARDA programme and the federal contribution was 37.5 percent for this one project.

HYDRAULIC PROJECTS

Since 1950 when the first hydraulic project, the Ingersoll channel, was undertaken by the upper Thames authority until the end of December 1970, 466 projects large and small have been carried out or are under way. With this large number under review, it is obvious that it would not be feasible to describe each one. Each large dam, because of its importance for flood control, will be dealt with briefly. The other dams will be dealt with in three groups: small dams built between 1950 and 1970; dams built under the water supply reservoirs programme from 1964 to 1970; and little dams built between 1950 and 1970. The remaining projects, because of their diversity, will be dealt with in small groups or singly.

Large dams (seven units)
The Fanshawe Dam and reservoir situated on the Thames river, five miles upstream from the city of London, was built by the Upper Thames River Conservation Authority at a cost of $5.3 million primarily to prevent flooding in the city. It

The Ingersoll diversion channel, 1947, one of the first channel improvements attempted by any authority. This channel provides an alternative route for the flood waters of the Thames River, thereby disposing of the water downstream before it can inundate the town's industries and homes.

Fanshawe Dam on the Thames River northeast of London was the first flood-control dam built by a conservation authority. The photograph shows the dam on opening day, 28 September 1953.

was not designed as a summer flow reservoir. Immediately behind the dam is a permanent lake, one-half mile wide and five miles long, which was built as a focal point for a large variety of recreation facilities. The storage capacity of the lake and the reservoir is 38,880 acre-feet. (An acre-foot of water is the amount required to cover an area of one acre to a depth of one foot.) The dam was officially opened on 18 September 1953.

The Luther Marsh Dam and reservoir is located in Luther Township at the headwaters of the Grand River and named after a marsh approximately 5,000 acres in size, which in former years was drained, farmed unsuccessfully and periodically burned. The Grand River Conservation Commission acquired about 4,900 acres of this area and in 1953 built a dam for $240,000 at the south end of the marsh on Black Creek which flows into the Grand River. Its primary purpose is for summer flow, but in addition, and because of the shallow depth of the reservoir, it has become an excellent haven for wildlife. The storage capacity is 10,000 acre-feet.

The Conestoga Dam and reservoir is situated on the Conestoga River, a tributary of the Grand River, near the hamlet of Glen Allan. It was built by the Grand River Conservation Commission and finished in 1957 at a cost of $3.8 million. The primary purpose is flood control and summer flow below the confluence of the Conestoga and the Grand. The storage capacity of the reservoir is 45,000 acre-feet.

The Gordon Pittock Dam and reservoir, located on the south branch of the Thames River approximately one-half mile upstream of the Highway 59 crossing in the city of Woodstock, was built at a cost of $4.9 million by the Upper Thames River Conservation Authority in 1966. Built primarily to prevent flooding in the city, it also provides a lake for recreation and limited low-flow augmentation. The reservoir, which has a capacity of 13,350 acre-feet, forms a lake four miles long.

The Wildwood Dam and reservoir is situated on Trout Creek, a tributary of the Thames River approximately three miles upstream from the town of St Marys where the two rivers meet. It was built by the Upper Thames River Conservation Authority, cost $3 million and was formally opened 15 June 1967. Its primary purpose is flood control for St Marys and London and summer flow for the north branch of the Thames and the main river below London. The capacity of its reservoir is 20,080 acre-feet.

Claireville Dam and reservoir, situated near the hamlet of Claireville on the west branch of the Humber River, was built by the Metropolitan Toronto and Region Conservation Authority and is designed to operate in conjunction with the Ebenezer Dam and reservoir to be constructed approximately two miles upstream. Its purpose is flood control and recreation. It cost $5.2 million, has a permanent lake of 120 acres and a capacity of 700 acre-feet with a total reservoir capacity of 6,000 acre-feet. The dam and reservoir were officially opened on 16 September 1964.

Parkhill Dam and reservoir is situated at the northern limits of the town of Parkhill. It consists of two structures, the larger North Dam located across the valley of the main Parkhill Creek and the South Dam, which contains the spillway and control structure situated on a tributary stream. The dam and associated Cameron-Gillies drain diversion was built by the Ausable River Conservation Authority to prevent flooding in the town of Parkhill and the rich market gardening

The Claireville Dam on the Humber was the first dam constructed by the Metropolitan Toronto and Region Conservation Authority. It provides flood control and recreation for the whole metropolitan area.

lands downstream, summer flow for Parkhill Creek, and emergency water supply for the town of Parkhill. The storage is 9,500 acre-feet and it cost $826,000. It was officially opened on 5 September 1969.

Small dams built 1950–70 (eighty-four units)
These vary in size depending on the purpose for which they were built. Several have been constructed in conservation areas to provide a small amount of flood control and to form a lake for recreation. A few have been built within the confines of urban areas providing some flood control and at the same time forming an attractive lake.

An interesting project was the building of the Second Depot Lake Dam on the Napanee at the outlet of a chain of lakes twelve miles in length. This raised the water level and created a reservoir to provide control in times of high flows and greatly improved summer flow; the town of Napanee, downstream, obtains its water supply from the river. A similar project, the Rankin River Dam, was built in 1961 by the Sauble Valley Conservation Authority. It controls a waterway eight miles long and includes three lakes and their adjoining rivers, which, for the most part, have marshy shores. The dam has created an excellent wildlife area.

On the Laurentian Shield, the Lingham Lake Dam on the Moira River was built by lumbermen to form a lake of 1,970 acres. The dam increased the flow in the river below and assisted the lumbermen to float their logs. It was rebuilt by the Moira River Conservation Authority in 1960 and the reclaimed lake provides welcome summer flow.

In this group, also, is the Black Creek Retardation Dam built by the Metropolitan Toronto and Region Conservation Authority on Black Creek in 1960. It is built entirely of rock (talus and riprap) without an impervious core or cut-off wall. It was

A 'retardation' dam on Black Creek, a tributary of the Humber. This kind of dam, constructed of large stone blocks, does not restrain flood waters but merely holds them back – retards them – and forces the waters to percolate through the structure at a slower, less damaging rate. This dam was built by the MTRCA in 1959.

designed so that at the time of flooding the excess flow is held back, and only the amount of water which the channel below can contain passes through a small concrete opening without gates and the interstices of the dam.

Small water supply reservoirs
The year 1963 was one of severe drought in Ontario, particularly in the southwest, where farmers were forced to haul water for cattle. As a result it was recommended that the government's assistance to conservation authorities for the construction of water supply reservoirs be increased from the existing 50 percent grant. The new policy made provincial assistance available to authorities in the form of a grant of as much as 100 percent of the cost of a dam and reservoir including land acquisition. Twenty-five percent of the grant was to be repaid within thirteen years after the initiation of the project. The first three years of the repayment period were interest free. The remainder was to be paid within the last ten years with interest at a specified rate. The programme was also made available to municipalities which lay outside of constituted conservation authorities and was to run until 1967.

However, in 1967, the federal government introduced the Agricultural Rehabilitation and Development Act (ARDA), which was intended to assist farmers and other rural people. The federal government agreed to put Ontario's small water supply reservoir programme under this act and make grants equal to the province's contribution. As a result the government of Ontario extended the period of its small reservoir programme to the end of 1971 and for the last four years the government of Canada paid 37.5 percent of the cost of dams built under this programme.

Some of these dams were fairly large 'small' dams and included such structures

The Christie Dam on Spencer Creek was built in 1970 by the Hamilton Region Conservation Authority under the provincial government's small reservoir programme.

The George S. Jarrett Dam (formerly the Maley Dam) on Junction Creek at Sudbury.

as the Maley Dam on Junction Creek near Sudbury and the Milne Dam at Markham on the Rouge River in the Metropolitan Toronto and Region Conservation Authority.

A complete list of small water supply reservoirs follows:

CONSERVATION AUTHORITY	SMALL WATER SUPPLY RESERVOIR
Big Creek	Lehman
	Hay Creek
	Vittoria
	Deer Creek
	Norwich
Cataraqui	Buell Creek
	Upper Cataraqui
Catfish	Springwater
Credit	Mono
	Orangeville
Crowe	Crowe Bridge weir
	Wollaston
Grand	Columbia
	Mill Creek
	Victoria Mills
	Laurel Creek
	Chicopee
	Shade's Mill
	New Dundee
Halton	Mountsberg
	Scotch Block
Hamilton	Valens
	Christie
Holland	Rogers
	Scanlon Creek
Junction	Kelly Lake
	Robinson
	Nepahwin
	Clarabelle
	Frood
	Laurentian
	Perch Lake
	Southeast shore
	Maley
Lakehead	Neebing weir
Lower Thames	Sharon Creek
Maitland	Howson
Metro Toronto	Milne
	Stouffville
Moira	Lime Lake
	Moira Lake
	Stoco Lake (two dams)
	Moira Seasonal Dam
	Deerock Lake
Napanee	Hardwood
	Third Depot Lake
	Lonsdale weir
Niagara	Virgil (two dams)
	Oswego
	Binbrook

CONSERVATION AUTHORITY	SMALL WATER SUPPLY RESERVOIR
Nottawasaga	New Lowell
	Utopia
Prince Edward	Consecon
Rideau	Haggart
	Richmond weir
Sauble	Skinner marsh
South Nation	Russell
Sydenham	Petrolia
	Campbell
	Coldstream
	Morragh
	Warwick
Upper Thames	Springbank
Whitson	Chelmsford

Little dams built 1950–70

These include reclaimed or existing mill ponds. In some cases where the old mills are still standing they have been rehabilitated to re-create a centre of activity. Many are located in small conservation areas of a few acres close to a town or village and are a focal point for community recreation both summer and winter. They have no flood-control potential but add to the beauty of the area and provide, in some cases, a limited amount of aquatic activities. These are:

CONSERVATION AUTHORITY	LITTLE DAM
Ausable	Morrison
	Exeter
Big Creek	Backus
	Sutton
Credit	Fairy Lake
Grand	Floradale
Halton	Burn's Mills
Maitland	Gorrie
	Wingham
Mattagami	Gillies Lake
Moira	Lingham Lake
	Flinton
Napanee	Second Depot Lake
	Colebrook
	Ardens
North Grey	Bognor
Otonabee	Hope
	Lang Mill
Rideau	Bellamy
Saugeen	Durham
Sault Ste Marie	Fort Creek

This dyke at Walkerton was built by the Saugeen Valley Conservation Authority in 1967 to give additional protection to homes and industries located on the river's banks.

One little dam deserves honourable mention. In a part of the province which is noted for its marl, Shallow Lake with a surface area of approximately 300 acres was drained by blasting a channel through the bedrock and the bed was used as a quarry for the manufacturing of cement. This occurred some years ago. In 1961, the Sauble Valley Conservation Authority built a control dam on Parkhead Creek at the outlet of the lake for the modest cost of $1,450, refilling the lake which has again become ideal for fish and wildlife.

Other projects
One kind of project which has proved effective and which approaches the cost of a good size dam is the building of a flood channel to lead flood waters safely through, or around, urban centres or other valuable properties.

In one instance, a bridge on the Saugeen River was threatened by flood waters; if the bridge had been washed out travel in part of Brant township would have been seriously disrupted. The bridge was made stable again by channel improvement and bank stabilization work undertaken by the conservation authority.

In another case, the town of Walkerton was bisected by the Saugeen River and much of the business section and older residential areas were periodically flooded; the danger of flooding was averted by channel improvements and building of dykes. This programme was carried out over a period of years and was planned to take advantage of material available from several large earth excavation projects in the town at a substantial savings in cost.

In most rivers, silting, especially in the lower region, becomes a problem. In a few cases where this has become serious dredging has been carried out by the authority. These include the dredging of the lower Don River by the former Don

One man died when the backyards of these homes, sodden with spring rain and melting snow cover, slumped into the valley of Taylor Creek in 1966. Investigation proved the backyards had been built up with unstable fill that collapsed in the wet conditions.

Valley Conservation Authority in 1956 and the two projects of the Ausable River Conservation Authority at Port Franks and Grand Bend in 1950 and 1958 respectively.

In the small village of Wellesley which clusters around a mill pond, and in the city of Stratford which has a forty-four acre lake as its chief landscape attraction, the problem was removing the silt which had accumulated for years. At these two sites, the Grand River and Upper Thames River Conservation Authorities in 1957 and 1964 undertook the removal of the silt and debris and restored the ponds to their former attractiveness. Similar projects were carried out in the town of Mitchell by the Upper Thames River Conservation Authority in 1963 and at Fairy Lake in the town of Acton by the Credit Valley Conservation Authority in 1968.

Riverbank erosion is a serious problem along most rivers in Ontario. Many authorities have done preventative work of this type by the use of riprap on small rivers and gabions and sheet piling walls on the large ones. As a matter of interest the first gabion work undertaken in Ontario – if not all of Canada – was the bank stabilization work carried by the Grand River Conservation Authority at Bridgeport in 1957. This installation consisted of four large groynes constructed at the toe of a steep eroding bank where a large building and several homes were in danger of toppling into the river. Numerous riverbank erosion control projects employing various methods of protection have been undertaken by the conservation authorities throughout Ontario, particularly the Lower Thames and Sydenham Valley Conservation Authorities in Southwestern Ontario.

Also, a number of authorities have undertaken valley-slope stabilization work, mainly in urban areas where homes have been threatened by undermining. Notably among those are the St Lucie and Troutbrook Drive projects carried out by the Metropolitan Toronto and Region Conservation Authority in 1968 and the Medway Creek slope-stabilization project of the Upper Thames River Conservation Authority in 1968.

Finally, two successful examples of ground-water recharging or 'water spreading,' as it is sometimes called, have been carried out. The first was by the Catfish Creek Conservation Authority at Aylmer in 1954, where spring runoff, which normally caused nuisance flooding in the town, was directed to an underground aquifer through a large diameter borehole to replenish the ground-water supply which had dropped more than twenty feet due to excessive pumping. The second was the water-spreading project of the Upper Thames River Conservation Authority at Fanshawe, where approximately 5 million gallons per day were pumped from the reservoir to a series of small kettle ponds located over gravel beds supplying water to the city of London.

In the hamlet of Goodwood, which was periodically flooded due to lack of drainage, the Metropolitan Toronto and Region Conservation Authority installed (in 1958) a large capacity pump to lift the excess water over the height of land and discharge it into the headwaters of Duffin Creek.

Included in the above mentioned projects are a number of projects carried out by the authorities in Northern Ontario. At present there are five authorities in the north: Junction Creek, Whitson Valley, Mattagami, Sault Ste Marie and Lakehead Region. All of these, particularly the Junction Creek, have been active in flood and erosion control and water conservation work. The Lakehead Region Conservation Authority has completed several channel improvements while the authority at Sault Ste Marie has built the Fort Creek Dam and has plans for the construction of multi-million dollar channel improvements under way.

Flood problems in the town of Timmins and Mountjoy Township have largely been eliminated by the projects carried out by the Mattagami Valley Conservation Authority. These projects include extensive channel improvements on Town Creek and the removal of homes from the flood plain. These are on-going programmes which have been under way since 1962 and are being completed as funds permit.

To further indicate the magnitude and monetary value of all these projects which have been carried out over the period 1950–70, the total expenditure amounts to more than $60 million.

4
Forests for the Future

The Ganaraska authority was the first to undertake reforestation on a large scale. In spite of the fact that the watershed, and particularly the town of Port Hope, had been plagued with floods over the years, it was decided to postpone the building of dams until a more convenient date and to proceed, instead, with reforestation.

The authority at that time included only parts of five townships and the town of Port Hope; it seemed, therefore, more appropriate to undertake a scheme which would not be too great a load on the municipalities and which could be financed each year as the work progressed. In making this decision the authority was guided in part by the Ganaraska report which stated, 'The most important conservation measure recommended is the establishing of a forest on the northerly part of the watershed on what is known as the interlobate moraine. This moraine is a long narrow area of sandy loam and gravel which extends throughout a part of Southern Ontario, commencing in York County and reappearing again in Ontario County and continuing through Durham and Northumberland Counties. The area included in the proposed forest is approximately 20,000 acres, much of which is plantable land and woodland, with here and there, farms of low productive value.'

Then, too, reforestation on a large scale was familiar to the men of the Ganaraska. In the United Counties of Northumberland and Durham where the watershed is situated, some of the pioneer work in reforestation had been carried out. It was on the farm of Francis Squair in Darlington Township that the first woodlot was planted under the free-tree programme for farmers, inaugurated by the Ontario government in 1905. In 1922 the forest tree nursery of the Department of Lands and Forests was established at Orono, just west of the Ganaraska boundary; the nursery contains excellent plantations of different species of forest trees. In 1924 one of the earliest county forests was established in Northumberland County, followed a few years later by a similar forest in Durham County.

In commencing this work, the Ganaraska was breaking new ground as far as the authorities were concerned, and one of the first decisions to be made was how the planting should be organized. It was a simple matter to acquire the land, but the big

In the 1920s and 1930s vast areas of formerly productive farmlands turned into hillocks of blowsand through destructive farming practices and ignorance of conservation techniques. Such scenes are – happily – a thing of the past.

problem was to finance the required technical staff to supervise the planting and to manage the forest as it grew to the anticipated size of 20,000 acres.

The county forest programme in the Department of Lands and Forests had proved successful, and it seemed that the best solution would be to bring the Ganaraska forest under the same agreement as that used for county forests. When this solution was suggested to the Honourable Dana Porter, he discussed it with the Honourable G.W. Thompson, minister of lands and forests, and the necessary arrangements were promptly made. Moreover, not only would the Ganaraska forest come under the same type of agreement but *all* authorities' forests could be included.

As the negotiations proceeded, someone added icing to the cake. Whereas the agreement with counties provided that they must acquire and pay the full price of the land, after which it would be transferred to the Department of Lands and Forests for planting and management, the authorities were given a grant of 50 percent of the cost of the land.

The first tree in the Ganaraska authority forest was planted on 14 May 1947 by the Honourable Dana Porter. In the 1947 December number of *Conservation*, the newsletter of the Ontario Conservation and Reforestation Association, is an interesting picture with the caption: 'The Honourable Dana Porter, minister of planning and development, when planting a tree in the Ganaraska forest, threw off his coat and vest, which action is symbolic, perhaps, of what is to take place on the Ganaraska and other Ontario watersheds.'

In the early years of reforestation, the emphasis was on planting waste lands of Ontario – areas of blowsand, undeveloped cut-over pine barrens with old stumps still standing, and abandoned pasture of light soil which today constitute some of the valuable tobacco lands of the province.

A handsome stand of sugar maple and beech on the Humber watershed.

The policy of acquiring young stands of hardwoods, or timber of large sizes, with plantable land for county forests was slow in taking hold. Where such wooded areas did occur the owner, in most cases, insisted on selling his whole farm, bush *and* open land. The Ganaraska authority soon ran into this problem because there was much woodland interspersed with the plantable land on the proposed Ganaraska forest. It seemed reasonable to the authority, that if it purchased land which contained mature timber or thrifty young hardwoods, that some recompense should be allowed for these areas which had, in effect, reforested themselves. Accordingly, the Ganaraska authority appealed to the province for consideration with the result that Ontario agreed to make a grant to the authority equal to the value of the standing timber, the value of which to be calculated by foresters from the Department of Lands and Forests. This new policy was a great stimulus to the acquiring of authority forests.

In 1970 twenty-three authorities had forests with a total of 84,739 acres managed by the Department of Lands and Forests. These varied in size from the smallest, with 145 acres, to the Moira with 16,517 acres and the Saugeen with 12,627 acres. The size of the forest depends on the area of suitable land available in the authority, the cost of such land and the length of the time the authority has been engaged in such work.

Four of the largest forests occupy land which is largely unsuitable for agriculture; others include sandy areas which at one time supported forests of white pine and were abandoned as farms; at least one has a considerable amount of tax delinquent land; a few are small tracts of standing timber; another was acquired to protect a large swamp sparsely covered with trees at the headwaters of the Thames River; and at the Lakehead, one comprises a swamp of black spruce and cedar. But the most outstanding addition to the authority forest programme was the acquisition of two of the last stands of southern hardwoods in the Lake Erie district, Backus woods on the Big Creek and White's bush on Catfish Creek. Both deserve special mention.

The enlargement of the original Big Creek Valley Conservation Authority in 1954 brought within its area the John C. Backus property in South Walsingham, not far from Port Rowan, which presented an outstanding opportunity for an authority forest. In the summer of 1955, while the conservation survey was in progress, Evans Knowles, then chairman of the authority, was able to interest the owners in public acquisition of their holdings; a total of 698 acres, including an old mill built in 1798, was purchased for $98,000. The survey crew estimated the value of the merchantable timber, and a provincial grant on the timber value, together with the normal grant on land acquisition, made it possible for this relatively small authority to acquire an outstanding property.

The Backus woods comprise one of the few large tracts of deciduous forest in Ontario. It contains fine specimens of such southern species as tulip trees and black gum along with the associated minor flora, which gives considerable botanical interest to the property. Although it does not contain as many large mature trees as the well-known White's bush near Aylmer, the Backus woods covers a much larger area with considerable oak, pine, hard maple, beech and soft maple now approaching maturity. Now that this property is an authority forest, it is available for those with a particular botanical interest and those who just wish to admire the beauties of the southern forests of Ontario as the pioneers saw them.

White's bush, in the Catfish Creek Conservation Authority in Elgin County, is the finest continuous stretch of southern hardwoods forest in Ontario east of Rondeau Park. Both the amateur naturalist and the scientist have been attracted by the great variety of plants and animals found in this woodland and around the Springwater Pond, which provides excellent swimming, canoeing and fishing. Among the giant hardwoods are magnificent beech, red oak, white oak, black oak, the occasional yellow poplar (tulip tree), hickory and cottonwood. Many of the trees, two to three feet in diameter, are more than 200 years old. Above all tower the stately white pines, some of them 125 feet high. These trees were well established when the first settlers arrived in this area. The 369-acre tract contains many lesser plants of interest – including such shrubs as the flowering dogwood and the sassa-

White's bush on Catfish Creek as it looked in 1950. This is one of the finest stands of climax forest in Ontario; some of the pines reach more than 125 feet in height and were mature trees when European explorers first came to the province.

fras – and provides a home for a great variety of animal and bird life, including such species as the hooded warbler which is rarely found this far north.

Such a fine stand of timber was, of course, attractive to the lumbermen as well as the naturalist, and there were some anxious moments before White's bush was finally secured for public use. Some cutting is necessary to salvage trees which would otherwise die and be wasted, and to encourage new growth so that the forest can be perpetuated. However, wholesale slashing of the bush would destroy its nature entirely.

Public acquisition of White's bush was recommended in the Catfish Creek conservation report prepared by the Conservation Branch and published in 1951, shortly after the conservation authority was formed. In 1955 the Federation of Ontario Naturalists issued a report urging public acquisition of the area. However, this was a large undertaking for so small an authority, and while intermittent negotiations were carried on with the owner, Fred White, the transaction had not been completed at the time of his death in 1962. The matter then became urgent as the estate had to be liquidated.

The authority took immediate action and with the aid of a generous grant from the province to cover the value of the standing timber, and with the efforts of F.G. Jackson, head of the forestry section of the branch, was able to secure the property. Ninety-three acres including Springwater Pond are now operated by the authority for public use and the remaining 276 acres are managed for the authority by the Ontario Department of Lands and Forests under a long-term agreement. This magnificent forest reserve, two miles south of Orwell on Highway 3 between Aylmer and St Thomas, now forms a memorial to Fred White and all those who worked for its preservation; it is enjoyed by an increasing number of visitors every year.

AUTHORITY FORESTS AS OF 31 DECEMBER 1970

Authority	Forest established	Acres
Ausable	1952	4,396
Big Creek	1955	3,757
Catfish	1954	627
Central Lake Ontario	1963	295
Crowe	1963	200
Ganaraska	1947	8,736
Grand	1956	5,768
Hamilton	1962	12
Lakehead	1958	1,825
Lower Thames	1964	308
Maitland	1956	949
MTRCA	1952	1,673
Moira	1953	16,517
Napanee	1954	6,749
Niagara	1963	186
North Grey	1958	6,948
Otonabee	1963	1,820
Otter	1957	1,517
Sauble	1959	3,818
Saugeen	1953	12,627
South Nation	1962	2,502
Sydenham	1965	150
Upper Thames	1954	3,359
Total		84,739

In 1949 the Grand River Conservation Commission started planning for the Conestoga Dam and applied to the two senior governments for financial assistance on the same basis as that given for the Shand and Luther Marsh Dams – 37.5 per cent from each. The two governments agreed to make the contributions but in addition, the federal government requested the commission to submit a plan of ancillary conservation measures which among other projects must include the reforesting of thirty square miles of the Grand valley in twenty years. In terms of acreage, this meant approximately 1,000 acres per year would be reforested. In making this request Ottawa applied a broad definition to the word 'reforestation,' and did not confine it strictly to plantable land but included swamp forests, marsh-land, river-valley slopes, standing timber and all areas which, in the aggregate, would have some bearing on runoff in the Grand River basin.

Although the request came as a surprise to the commission, it was certainly not unreasonable; the projects which the government requested were ancillary to the problems of water control and water conservation which the commission was formed to solve. Yet logical though it was, the condition presented the commission with what seemed to be an insurmountable task. It was evident that the advisers to the minister in Ottawa had read the Grand Valley conservation report, prepared by the Conservation Branch, and from which they got their figures for recommending the size of the area to be reforested; at the same time, Ottawa confused the jurisdiction of the commission with that of the authority. The commission, it will be recalled, was formed to build structures to prevent floods and increase the summer flow in the Grand River and was composed of representatives from only eight urban municipalities; on the other hand, the authority included all seventy-two municipalities and had jurisdiction over the whole river valley for all kinds of conservation schemes.

It was evident that something had to be done to break the impasse so that the commission could get funds for the Conestoga Dam from the federal government. The commission approached the authority to inquire if it would assume responsibility for carrying out the reforestation. The authority agreed providing the commission would pass the resolution: 'The Grand River Conservation Commission will enter into an agreement with the authority that no lands required for the construction of the Conestoga Dam and reservoir, or lands for future projects of a similar nature, shall be acquired, utilized or disposed of without prior approval of the chief conservation engineer of the Department of Planning and Development.' The commission agreed.

In the spring of 1958 it came to the attention of the authority executive that a large cottage subdivision had been laid out on surplus lands of the Conestoga. As the Conservation Branch had not been requested to approve the use of the land for this purpose, the executive asked for a meeting with the commission for an explanation. The meeting was held in Kitchener and resulted in a stalemate. During the discussion, the chairman of the authority asked the secretary-treasurer of the commission why the cottage subdivision had been proceeded with contrary to the agreement as set forth in the resolution. The secretary denied that the commission had entered into any such agreement. As a consequence, the authority withdrew its support from the commission's reforestation programme.

In retrospect, it was unfortunate that the commission broke faith with the authority because here was an opportunity for the two groups to work together in establishing what might have become the largest authority forest in the province. However, it should be recorded that the commission, in spite of this delinquency, was much interested in reforestation on its own properties. In 1943, immediately after the completion of the Shand Dam, it began planting on surplus land bordering the reservoir. The same was true with the Luther Marsh Dam in 1952 and the Conestoga in 1959. From the commencement of this work until 1966, the number of trees planted on these three properties totalled 5 million. In the early years, trees were obtained from the Department of Lands and Forests but in 1956 the commission established its own tree nursery.

There were no authority forests when this work started, consequently there were no grants from the government – the commission had to arrange its own financing. This it did by levies on the member municipalities and rentals from cottage sites on the margins of Bellwood Lake above the Shand Dam. This financial independence gave the commission a freedom of action which placed it in an enviable position compared with the authorities, and this method of financing continued until the commission and the authority were amalgamated in 1966.

Early in the work of the authorities much emphasis was placed on partnerships with landowners to improve their properties by means of conservation projects.

One of the earliest tree-planting machines used in Ontario is shown in operation on the lands of the Moira River Conservation Authority in the 1950s.

One type of work which lent itself readily in this respect was reforestation. To assist, some of the authorities purchased tree-planting machines, and, under the supervision of authority personnel, planted trees on private land at cost. The trees were purchased from lands and forests and made ready on the planting site by and at the expense of the owner. Figures are not available for the number of trees planted by all authorities which have this programme of assistance, but they run to many millions. One good example is the Metropolitan Toronto and Region Conservation Authority, which from 1957 to 1970 under this programme has assisted in planting 4 million trees.

Although private tree planting is not so spectacular as some other types of work – these plantations are not seen usually by the general public – nevertheless it has given thousands of people within the authorities and beyond an opportunity of making a contribution to the overall conservation effort in Ontario. Moreover, there is something very satisfying in planting a small plantation of forest trees on one's own property. There is pure pleasure in watching trees grow from the time they are so small that a dozen or more can be held in one hand until they become tall and straight and suitable for a Christmas tree or a flagpole, or yield wood for the fireplace. The planting of trees does something to a man. It inflates his ego in a nice way, and over the years, as he views the result of his handwork, he can truthfully say to himself: 'I, too, am a conservationist.'

In recent years, as is well known, the Dutch elm disease has destroyed an incalculable number of trees throughout Ontario – and the end is not yet in sight. From the time of settlement the elm has been one of the most admired trees on the provincial landscape. To replace these and improve the rural landscape generally – and also to grow shrubs for food cover for wildlife – the Metropolitan Toronto and Region Conservation Authority, a leader in this important work, established its own nursery in 1957. The trees supplied from it include some well known in the

Tree-planting programmes initiated by the conservation authorities have been so successful that several authorities have established their own nurseries to provide reliable, inexpensive stock.

average woodlot such as ash, basswood, white birch, butternut, black cherry, hard, silver and red maple, red oak, walnut and a few exotics.

Under the assistance programme for such planting, a landowner with a minimum of ten acres can obtain trees approximately five feet in height and have them planted for a nominal sum. For wildlife cover and food, nineteen shrubs most suitable for the purpose have been selected, and where the landowner has at least ten acres, one hundred shrubs will be supplied and planted for a nominal sum. Since the programme started there has been a steady increase in the demand for such assistance. To 1970, 37,420 replacement trees and 17,365 shrubs were planted.

5
The Life-giving Carpet

'Soil erosion is part and parcel of mankind [reads in part the 1950 report of the Ontario Select Committee on Conservation]. Life depends on food and, therefore, on productive land. Wherever climate and vegetation had laid down a few inches of top soil, man began to multiply. Each and every civilization has been poised precariously on this thin, life-giving carpet. It covers only a small part of the earth's surface, yet without it humanity would be reduced to a few bands of nomadic fishermen and hunters.'

When the Conservation Branch was established there was much raising of eyebrows among the echelons of some of the old departments of the government. In agriculture and lands and forests particularly, there were questions as to what this new branch was up to. There were rumours that it was planning to emulate the United States Soil Conservation Service – mischievous talk with no foundation. To some the establishment of a new branch carried the connotation that it might become the senior branch in the government dealing with the burgeoning field of conservation. However, when the Conservation Branch commenced to function, it was amply demonstrated that its duties had to do with assisting the authorities with their many problems within the framework of the act. On 1 January 1962 when the branch was transferred to lands and forests, it was given a more explicit title: the Conservation Authorities Branch.

After passage of the US Soil Conservation Service Act in 1935 and the subsequent programme of the Soil Conservation Service, many new ideas in soil and water conservation filtered into Ontario and our branch personnel wondered how many were applicable to our province. Thus, when the Conservation Branch carried out a land-use survey for an authority it was with the purpose of indicating troublesome areas where currently acceptable methods and some of the new methods of soil and water conservation might be practised. Therefore, the contribution which the authorities made towards this important work was one of demonstration. With the assistance of the agricultural representatives of the Department of Agriculture, the soils department of the Ontario Agricultural College, local agricultural groups and

Every year several feet of arable farmland sloughed off in the spring and flowed down the course of the Stewart gully on the Ausable River watershed. In 1967 the authority constructed this set of restraining 'stairs' which retards the flow of the water and allows the silt to settle out before it is swept downstream and lost.

farmers who cooperated by employing these new methods, many valuable demonstrations were provided in the province.

In all these demonstrations, leadership was given by the land-use advisory boards. After a farm plan prepared by the soils department was implemented, the farm was used as an example for other farmers. The same was also true of demonstrations of crop rotations, cover crops, improved pasture, contour cultivation, strip-cropping, grassed waterways, gully control, drainage, woodland management, farm ponds, and windbreaks. In most of these undertakings grants were made to the landowner and in others the authority underwrote the project's cost.

Also, it should be recorded that on several conservation areas which had suitable land for agriculture, many of the above farming techniques were demonstrated. One of special interest is a pasture farm, which was described by the Saugeen valley authority:

The pasture farm, comprising approximately 200 acres, was bought by the authority as part of a plan for a conservation area. Believing that good grass cover is an excellent soil and water conservation measure and that a need for pasture improvement existed in the district, the land use advisory board visualized the use of ninety-six acres of good agricultural land on this farm as a means of demonstrating various ways of improving pasture. It was the hope that through experimentation certain worthwhile information could be passed along to the farmers of the district in the hope that they, too, would incorporate pasture improvement as a sound soil and water conservation measure into their farm programmes.

The Ontario Department of Agriculture, and, in particular, the Ontario Beef Pasture Improvement Committee, were the main contributors in assisting the authority to set up this

To help communicate the message of conservation various authorities established demonstration farms practising approved techniques. Here, in the 1950s, is one of the first demonstration pasture farms established by the Saugeen Valley Conservation Authority.

Conservation authorities enlisted the help of soil experts from the Ontario Agricultural College to help farmers plan the wise use of their land. With map in hand, an OAC expert explains the wisdom of crop rotation and strip-cropping (background) to a farmer and his young son.

Conservation authorities provided the first technical assistance for the construction of farm ponds in Ontario. This example is a by-pass pond.

demonstration pasture farm. They have conducted experiments on half the acreage devoted to pasture improvement as well as given advice to the authority who experiment on the other half.

In 1950 the authorities embarked on a programme to promote the building of farm ponds. The proposal for such a programme first appeared in the land-use section of the conservation report prepared for the Don Valley authority. Subsequently, this material with some added features was published as a twenty-eight-page bulletin. The value of farm ponds was set forth in the introductory paragraphs:

Water supply on farms in Southern Ontario is obtained from wells, streams, springs, ponds and cisterns. With the mechanization of farm operations, the improvements in sanitation and with larger and better herds, there is an increased demand for water. Supplies, on the other hand, are diminishing. Shallow wells often get their supply from 'perched' water tables which are rapidly disappearing and are not likely to be re-established. Deep wells and some shallow wells draw water from the permanent level of underground water. This, in many regions, has lowered considerably. Streams, springs and ponds are drying up or are being filled in, partly through mismanagement but largely from the gradual change in the physical features of the land which goes along with the change in land use.

Against this increased demand and diminished supply can be balanced one outstanding natural feature, namely, that Southern Ontario receives, on the average, thirty inches or more of rainfall in a year. Although there is often a lack of rainfall in the summer months there is an ample supply in winter and spring. The need, therefore, is to store some of this spring runoff by proper land use in the earth itself, and thus increase the ground-water supply and maintain summer flow in streams and springs.

Farm ponds are directly connected with soil conservation. The study of soil erosion in Southern Ontario reveals that the most important single remedy for arresting this insidious process is the establishing of good sod cover. This, in turn, would provide a considerable increase of grazing land. One of the biggest obstacles to establishing improved pasture on eroding land is the lack of watering places for herds. Properly managed springs, streams and natural ponds give the cheapest and most reliable supply of water. Small ponds offer the best form of management and provide reservoirs in time of drought.

The hazard of fire is becoming increasingly important with higher costs of buildings and equipment. Much is being done for fire protection by better organization and equipment, but fire-fighting apparatus requires ample supplies of water from which it can draw. Wells, in many instances, are inadequate for pumps. Natural supplies are not dependable and often remote from buildings. Therefore well-built ponds, favourably located, are much better sources for this purpose.

Many farmers know that good facilities for recreation are necessary to make farm life attractive to hired help and to their own children. Water, especially for swimming and skating, fishing and boating, can be the focus of recreational activities. There is increasing interest in ponds for this purpose.

Conservation aims at the creation of a balance between all living things, including wildlife population such as muskrats for commercial exploitation, game for hunting, fish for angling and certain species of birds and mammals for the control of pests. These purposes can be served by farm ponds or by well-managed natural streams, and in some instances they may be suitable for a combination of uses.

Recent spells of drought have created interest in irrigation. Ponds can serve a useful purpose in this regard, either by preservation of pasture or protecting a valuable cash crop. For example, a half-acre pond of average depth of four feet contains twenty-four 'acre-inches' of water, enough to cover a twelve-acre field with two inches of water. Throughout much of South-central Ontario there were in 1949 four weeks during June and July in which there was no rainfall at all in a period in which at least two inches could be expected as the average fall. Conveniently located, a pond of the above size could be used to take up this slack.

It is generally believed that any measures to hold water on the land would improve ground-water levels and summer flow in streams as well as mitigate flood conditions on rivers. It would take a good many ponds to effect a measurable improvement in this regard, but in view of the many other advantages in controlling surface flow of water it is not too much to hope that small ponds might become numerous enough to improve the whole situation materially.

Six types of farm ponds are described in the bulletin: the dug-out pond; the spring-fed pond; the by-pass pond; the run-off pond; the permanent stream pond; and the temporary pond. These types were illustrated by photographs and drawings, showing a plan, method of development and a section of the pond lengthwise.

In several cases the bulletin was published over the name of an authority with a message from the chairman. The bulletins were given wide circulation throughout the province; 40,000 were distributed to the authorities and 20,000, which carried the name of both departments, were printed for the Department of Agriculture.

While this programme was active, the authorities gave assistance to landowners, each authority deciding on its own policy of aid. There is no record of how many ponds were built under the programme but the number must have been well more than 5,000. One medium size authority, the Ausable which is largely rural, was instrumental in the digging of 647.

In 1956, the Department of Agriculture published a bulletin entitled, *Farm Ponds, Their Construction and Management*, after which the authorities ceased publishing theirs. In 1964, much to the regret of the authorities, this popular programme was transferred to the Department of Agriculture.

Reconnaissance land-use surveys made for the conservation reports, especially on a large authority, proved to be limited in their value because of the area covered. Accordingly, in 1952, at the request of some of the authorities, a programme of little valley studies was inaugurated by the branch so that the demonstration of better land use could be applied to smaller areas. Seven of these were carried out: Avon River, 1952, a tributary of the upper Thames River; Lutterell Creek 1953, which empties into the Speed River which is a tributary of the Grand River with a watershed area of 17,000 acres; King Creek 1954, a part of the east branch of the Humber River with a watershed of 20,177 acres; North Creek 1954, a tributary of Big Creek with a watershed of 12,500 acres; Black Creek 1956, a tributary of the Credit River with a watershed of 13,400 acres; Denfield Creek, a tributary of the Ausable River with a watershed of 18,000 acres; and Horner Creek which joins Kenney Creek to form Whiteman's Creek which flows into the Grand River between Brantford and Paris, with a watershed area of 44,000 acres.

The reports of these surveys were mimeographed in book form with maps and pictures and distributed to each landowner in the valley concerned. Three of the reports were printed for wider circulation and each of these had a facsimile of the farm plan of the landowner in the valley concerned prepared by the soils department of the Ontario Agricultural College. It also included a reproduction of an aerial photograph of the farm showing the different land classes in colour.

Following the distribution of the reports, meetings were held by the authorities to explain how the conservation measures could be implemented. To assist in this the US Soil Conservation Service loaned to the authorities the services of M.H. Cohee, one of their senior economists from Milwaukee. He spent the better part of a week in Southwestern Ontario discussing the soil and water progress of the service with groups and at public meetings.

The intent of this programme was well conceived, but to expect all the farmers in these little valleys to rearrange their farming business and conform with the recommendations of the reports without some financial assistance was an exercise in wishful thinking. One authority did consider giving financial assistance but on second thought declined; if assistance were extended to other little valleys in the authority the financial burden would have been astronomical. Nevertheless, the surveys and reports, especially the printed ones, served a useful purpose as a guide for the practice of conservation methods not only on the farms of the little valleys but throughout the whole authority.

The seventh little valley report, Horner Creek, was published in the Grand valley report of 1954, and in 1961 the area was resurveyed and the findings published in a separate report in 1962. In recent years (prior to 1971) the Grand River authority has been trying to activate a programme in its little valleys and has undertaken a public relations programme including assistance in planning for the farmers in the watershed.

6
The Other Inhabitants

When Kenneth Mayall joined the original technical staff of the Conservation Branch in the fall of 1945 to direct the work of wildlife and recreation, the branch had not decided what would be encompassed in the field of 'wildlife.' Accordingly, Mayall's first move was to discuss the matter with his friend and former colleague, Professor W.J.K. Harkness. Professor Harkness had been one of the promoters of the King Township survey and chairman of the King advisory board. At the time the Conservation Branch was formed he was director of the Ontario Fisheries Research Laboratories, University of Toronto, and when the Ontario Department of Game and Fisheries was amalgamated with the Department of Lands and Forests in 1946 he became its first chief. He was at that time the outstanding scientist in the field of fish and wildlife in Ontario.

Dr Harkness was asked to define the most significant work which could be carried out by the Conservation Branch and be of practical assistance to the conservation authorities. Harkness replied that, in his opinion, the most important work would be to classify all the streams of Southern Ontario, as to which were trout streams and which were not. He added that there had been a great deal of unnecessary stocking of streams with trout when, in fact, the streams were not suitable for the fish. He further recommended that the branch engage the services of Professor F.P. Ide of the University of Toronto as a consultant for this work.

Professor Ide had developed a technique for determining which streams were suitable environments for the support of trout. He collected and classified the insects found in the sand or gravel of a stream bed. After checking innumerable streams, he concluded that the brooks in which the nymphs and larvae (early stages) of mayflies, stoneflies, and caddisflies were found were also good streams for trout. The presence of these insects, he concluded, was a certain indication that the stream would not dry up in a summer drought; also, the presence of the insects indicated that the stream would always run cool – 75 degrees F. was known to be the maximum temperature endured by brook trout. So far as is known the Conservation Branch's method of classifying streams by their bottom fauna as devised by Dr Ide, was the only one in use in North America for twenty-five years. It seems that no other agency, either governmental of private, has seen fit to use this well-proven method, and a great deal of credit must go to Dr Ide for his patient research which led to a foolproof method.

Of course, it had long been known that waters which are polluted have very little oxygen in them and are commonly found to have vast numbers of pollution-tolerant organisms, usually midge larvae in huge numbers, to the exclusion of most other aquatic life. The Conservation Branch also used this information in classifying streams, and in locating the source of the pollution.

It was not possible to follow Dr Harkness' advice for all the streams in Ontario, but as each authority was formed, the conservation report included a map of the river system based on Dr Ide's method. These showed the different sections of the river in colours, indicating the condition in relation to suitability for fish. The maps were also available for distribution to the public.

The sources of pollution were recorded and passed on to the authority concerned. A few authorities carried out more extensive pollution surveys of their own and sent delegations to the government for assistance in cleaning up these offensive areas, but very little action was taken prior to the mid-fifties.

But better years were not far ahead. The public at last was awakening from its somnolence regarding pollution of the rivers and lakes, with the result that two important bodies were formed. In 1957 the Honourable Leslie Frost, premier of Ontario, established the Ontario Water Resources Commission with Dr A.E. Berry as general manager, and a new provincial statute was passed which covered the gamut of water problems. In 1960 the Great Lakes Institute was organized at the University of Toronto to investigate pollution and other pertinent matters in the lakes. Dr George B. Langford was the first director, which office he held until his retirement in 1966. During these years he did yeoman service through the media and by declaiming throughout the province the deteriorating conditions of some of the Great Lakes.

When the Conservation Branch was first established, little attention was paid to stream improvements for fish, but it was soon evident from the branch's surveys and American pioneering work that there were several ways in which streams and rivers could be made to produce more and better habitat. About 1953 Ken Mayall and Professor Antoon DeVos of the Ontario Agricultural College, Guelph, were given a 'royal' tour of Michigan by officials of the state government. They saw many different types of stream improvement, with digger logs, deflectors and – most important of all – bank-erosion control devices. A large number of streams were fenced, with anglers' paths along the streams. They also saw the famous Hunt Creek experiment station where electric shockers were used to stun fish so that they could be collected, counted, and returned to the stream.

Based on this visit, the Conservation Branch had a 300-volt shocker assembled, and the trout in many areas of Ontario were counted. This application of electrical shock techniques took place long before shockers came into general use in Ontario.

About the same time, a stream improvement competition was organized by the Grand Valley Conservation Authority for angling clubs, with a first prize of $1,000. The streams' quality was examined and judged before and after improvements were

Ontario was one of the first jurisdictions to use electric shock to conduct an accurate census of streams and stream fauna. Fish in the stream are stunned by the probes carried by the biologist in the middle; the stunned fish are netted, measured and sometimes tagged before being returned, unharmed, to the water. Note the long cord connecting the probes to the source of electricity.

One task undertaken by each authority was the improvement of all streams in its watershed for fish life. Deflectors like these, often built with old barn beams and railway ties, create pockets of still water for trout. These examples were built on a tributary of the Saugeen.

The Owen Sound Mill Dam on the Pottawatomi River was restored in 1959 by the North Grey Conservation Authority; to the right of the dam can be seen the first fish ladder constructed in Ontario.

made, by J.F. Gage of the Department of Lands and Forests, who also took into account the nature of the improvements themselves. The Burford Rod and Gun Club won the competition with excellent work on a small trout stream one mile east of Burford. Larger scale stream improvements, including riprap (interlocking stones) and a variety of deflectors were installed by the Metropolitan Toronto and Region Conservation Authority on trout streams in the Albion Hills conservation area, and in the Palgrave forest and wildlife area. Other authorities soon followed suit. Beams from old deserted barns were used for most of the deflectors which are put at curves in the stream where there is erosion: the deflectors move the water into a narrow channel which digs a hole providing excellent shelter for trout. Some discarded railroad ties and gabions were also used.

In the late 1950s, when Murray Johnson was seconded by the Conservation Branch to the Metropolitan Toronto and Region Conservation Authority as field officer, he gave splendid leadership in the work of wildlife there and to other authorities which were beginning projects in the field. At the Glen Haffy conservation area, an old building was converted into a hatchery for brook and rainbow trout which were used for stocking the streams and ponds of the authority; and – a second item of special interest – two major ponds at Glen Haffy were greatly improved with one reserved for children under 16 and the other for adults. The line-up of cars with fishermen, young and old, at the Glen Haffy conservation area on opening day of the trout season starts before 7 AM., although the gates are not opened until eight and the daily catch is limited to two trout per person.

At Mildmay, two miles south of Walkerton on a tributary of the Saugeen River, a stretch of trout stream was greatly improved for fish by the Saugeen authority and the area was restricted to fishing by school children.

The North Grey Conservation Authority incorporated the first concrete fish ladder for rainbow trout in the dam on the Pottawatomi River near Owen Sound. This stimulated the Department of Lands and Forests to have a larger fish ladder built on the Nottawasaga River near Alliston. The rainbow trout are counted (and some are tagged) as they go up this great river system. The stocking of rainbow trout is not an important feature of work in the province, and excellent catches are made. Rainbow trout, which grow to much larger size than brook or speckled trout, make their initial growth in the river systems where they are hatched, but make their main growth feeding on small fish in the Great Lakes, returning usually to their original stream to spawn.

In 1966, while attending a Fish and Wildlife conference in Quebec City, Ken Mayall learned about a new and improved design of fish ladder based on research conducted at Laval University, Quebec. Round holes in the baffles of fish ladders are arranged with mathematical precision so that there is slack current where fish can rest on their way up the fish ladder. The first fish ladder in Ontario of this design was built at Utopia Dam on a tributary of the Nottawasaga River by the Nottawasaga Conservation Authority, and has proved entirely successful. It is expected that this new design of fish ladder will become standard in Ontario.

Management of fishing in reservoirs and the tailwaters below dams has now begun. Normally, if the tailwaters are reasonably cool, rainbow trout are put in them. This is the situation now below the Shand Dam on the Grand River. The fishing there was exceptionally good in 1970. The reservoirs themselves may be stocked with bass or pickerel. Results from pickerel stocking have not been good in the Belwood reservoir. However, soon after Fanshawe Lake behind the Fanshawe Dam on the Thames River above London, was opened, pickerel grew very rapidly and there were excellent catches in this body of water.

During the middle of the 1950s, a popular outing in the spring was the junior trout-fishing days held by a number of authorities. The chief purpose was to introduce to young people the basic principles of conservation and the pleasures of angling. The arrangements varied slightly in different authorities but basically the routine and purpose were the same. The following excerpt from *Our Valley*, 1956, gives a good report on this type of outing.

The education and public relations advisory board in cooperation with the fish and wildlife advisory board of the Humber Conservation Authority held a junior trout-fishing day on 26 May 1956 in the Albion Hills conservation area. The project was an outstanding success. Five hundred Grade 8 children representing all school districts in the Humber watershed, who earned the opportunity to fish by submitting answers to three questions on fish conservation in the Humber River, were supervised by 135 representatives from rod and gun clubs. The Department of Lands and Forests stocked the streams with legalized trout. The catch was 223 trout and 340 chub and suckers. The cooperation of rod and gun clubs in providing transportation and instruction was gratifying and those who participated deserve special commendation for this most useful contribution to the conservation programme of the authority.

Several authorities have instituted junior anglers' days at which young fishermen, accompanied by fathers or teachers, try their luck unimpeded by adult competition. Some authorities have trout ponds exclusively reserved for junior anglers.

The establishment of large reservoirs such as those at Luther marsh, Mountsberg, Valens, Orangeville and many others to trap spring runoff, reducing floods and providing increased summer flow, has attracted vast numbers of migrant and nesting waterfowl. In some cases, emerging cattails and other less important vegetation have been turned to good use by the blasting of potholes in them with ANFO, a simple mixture of ammonium nitrate and fuel oil which explodes with a force roughly equal to dynamite at a fraction of the cost of dynamite. ANFO is very safe to use; a 50-lb bag can be detonated with a blasting cap and a single stick of dynamite. The conservation authorities were the first organizations to use this method, in Ontario; now it has become a commonplace. The most effective use of this method is to blast a circular pond with an island in the centre, relatively free from predators.

The recent discovery that the *maxima* or giant race of the Canada goose prefers to nest in Southern Ontario instead of in the Canadian Arctic as the smaller Canada goose does, has prompted the release of many of these birds in conservation authority waters. The young birds become 'imprinted' with the location where they have been raised and will return to the same nesting ground after they pair off in their second year. Canada geese are monogamous and if both birds survive the annual migration, they remain together for the rest of their lives. Divorce and polygamy are unknown in Canada geese and in that respect they set a good example to the human race.

The smaller song birds are not neglected by the conservation authorities. Winter-feeding programmes are carried out by most of the authorities, with millet, chicken feed and, of course, cracked corn for pheasants. Some authorities have also been sowing wild rice and buckwheat and introducing suitable aquatic plants for wildfowl in their impoundments.

At the first pioneer festival held at the Dalziel property in 1957, one of the

With the depletion of elm trees as a result of the Dutch elm disease infestation, nesting sites for wood ducks have also disappeared. Many authorities have been setting out artificial nesting boxes which approximate the hollow elms favoured by ducks.

exhibits was a display of shrubs and plants which produce food for birds. So much interest was aroused by this display that the Conservation Branch cooperated with the Humber authority and published a bulletin entitled *Some Plants Suitable for Attracting Wildlife*.

In its surveys of marshes the Conservation Branch found many areas which seemed to provide excellent food and cover for the most beautiful of all Ontario ducks, the wood duck. However, there were few wood ducks present in these marshes and it soon became apparent that the large old trees with nesting holes suitable for wood ducks were lacking. Many conservation authorities tried out various kinds of boxes, but most of them were used by starlings or not used at all. The biology section of the branch then produced two designs for satisfactory wood duck nesting boxes which could be fastened to posts driven into the mud of a marsh. These boxes were planned to discourage starlings by letting some light in at the back of the box, a feature which starlings don't like but wood ducks do. The designs have been sent to all conservation authorities and many of them have been erected (in winter, so as to be ready for the early arrival of the ducks). So far they have been successful. All are equipped with raccoon-proof, smooth, metal cylinders or inverted cones.

In some reservoirs (for example, the Wildwood reservoir on the Thames River above St. Marys) it has been found possible to cut off some part so that shallow water remains almost at the level of the spring runoff. These areas have been designated for the production of wildfowl and in some cases for hunting. Where hunting wildfowl is allowed in season, a large part of the reservoir is always kept as a game refuge, and in these sections there is always a 'baited' area where corn and other foods attractive to wildfowl are placed long before the open season for hunting so that there are always large concentrations of wildfowl by opening day. No one is allowed to hunt within 200 yards of a baited area. Hunting is strictly managed by the Department of Lands and Forests law-enforcement section. In the Valens reservoir in the Hamilton Region Conservation Authority, hunting is allowed only from 'duck blinds,' and these are rented by the day on a first-come, first-served basis. The blinds must be vacated by noon of any particular day.

Very large scale improvements to marshes are carried out to attract nesting ducks. The improvements include the clearing of woodlands in the immediate vicinity of the water and the replacement of them by unmowed hay which attracts black ducks and mallards. Behind the Luther Marsh Dam at the upper end of the Grand valley, the reservoir is 90 percent owned by the conservation authority and 10 percent by the Department of Lands and Forests. In this case, the marsh is managed by a joint committee consisting of three representatives of the authority's staff and three representatives of the department. This reservoir proved so attractive to wildfowl in its early years that enormous numbers of ducks came to it as a convenient stopping place on their spring and fall migrations. This, in turn, attracted many hunters and as there was only one road leading to it, it was possible to make an excellent census of the kinds and numbers of wildfowl taken from year to year. These, of course, were only a very small proportion of all the wildfowl present.

The Luther reservoir has been subjected to the same processes and effects which apply to most reservoirs where large areas of fertile soils are covered, and similarly to almost all of the beaver ponds in Southern Ontario. When first flooded, the great quantities of organic matter in the pond or reservoir give rise to an enormous increase in the fertility of the water. Useful aquatic plants develop and with them great numbers of minute, protein-bearing invertebrates develop and thrive. These are often the cause of rapid growth of young wildfowl hatched on or near the marsh. In the normal cycle of a beaver pond, for example, the bottom layer of sediments becomes covered with iron and manganese compounds which inhibit the release of phosphorous from the sediments. The water is then unproductive and dark, and the area is said to be 'stale' and of no use to wildlife. The solution of this problem is to drain the pond and let the sun heat it for at least one summer. There is then oxidation of the sediments at the bottom of the pond or reservoir and, when reflooded, the water becomes productive again.

This is what has happened to Luther marsh. The marsh, once the mecca of Southern Ontario hunters, now produces and harbours very few ducks. It will not return to its early condition until other flood-control and summer-flow dams are constructed, allowing most of Luther marsh to be left empty for a summer.

The conservation authorities have not neglected the naturalists. Besides bird-feeding stations already mentioned, the authorities have acquired many areas of rare and spectacular flowers or interesting associations of plants. Thus, for example, most of the Cavan bog near Peterborough, where many orchids grow, has been acquired by the Otonabee Region Conservation Authority. This programme has been greatly aided by financial assistance from the Nature Conservancy of Canada. The Conservation Branch of the provincial government had long since published a special report on this bog, noting, among other rare plants, the ram's head orchid. Similarly, the famous bog in the Cold Creek conservation area near Bolton has been

Boat Lake, on the Bruce peninsula, and Isaac and Sky Lakes above it, had been drained almost dry by manufacturing firms seeking the marl on the lake bottom. Marl, a fine white powder, is used in the manufacture of cement. The lowering of the lake level destroyed acres of favourite nesting sites of waterfowl. When the Sauble Valley Conservation Authority dammed the Rankin River (right foreground) the water levels rose and the water fowl returned to the lakes.

preserved for posterity. Visitors can visit this area only when accompanied by a member of the Metropolitan Toronto and Region Conservation Authority staff; a catwalk has been built over the areas containing the rarest plant species. Many of the plants found more commonly in northern bogs flower and fruit here successfully. Chief among these are the various species of cranberry. Similar catwalks to that mentioned have been built by the Grand River and Cataraqui Region Conservation Authorities.

For those interested in speliology, the study of caves, the Otonabee Region Conservation Authority has bought for public use the area containing the famous Warsaw caves. These lie on the banks of the Ouse River, in prehistoric times one of the major outlets of what is now known as the Trent River system.

One of the most comprehensive and useful series of changes in biological processes was that which occurred when the dam on the Rankin River (which is a tributary of the Sauble River at the base of the Bruce peninsula) was built by the Sauble authority. The dam had many effects. It immediately raised the level of Boat Lake which had been virtually inaccessible to boats in the summer. It greatly improved fishing in Boat Lake. It also raised the levels of water in Isaac and Sky Lakes and the channels between them so that boats could travel through the extensive marshes up from Boat Lake. It increased the waterfowl production of the marshes and the edges of Isaac and Sky Lakes, and also improved the hunting potential in all three lakes. So, there was a great increase in the natural resources of the area and also a greater annual yield of fish and wildlife, and this is one of the prime intentions of conservation.

To stimulate interest in wildlife, the Halton region authority imported a few buffalo to a large fenced enclosure near Milton. These proved a great attraction to the public. The herd has steadily increased and now numbers eighteen individuals with more expected annually. However, the Halton authority has many other important projects to its credit, including the raising of large numbers of pheasants and Chukar partridges every year and releasing them in the surrounding country.

All of the wildlife surveys of the branch have included accurate lists of all birds or mammals known to live in or migrate through the various regions or watersheds. Some readers may question the mention of mammals migrating in Southern Ontario. These are, of course, all bats, of which there are about twelve species in the province. They are of particular interest because they carry rabies and should not be handled at all. The exact location of nests of rare species of birds, such as the bald eagle, are not given in the reports because there are too many trigger-happy hunters who either do not know or do not care that the eagle is a protected species which it is illegal to shoot.

The wildlife section of the Conservation Branch changed its name to the biology section in 1966, as this section was responsible for the pollution sections in the survey reports. Detailed work in this field, including laboratory tests and field tests, was and is carried out with two ends in view. One is to locate the exact sources and amounts of pollutants; the second is to alert the general public and to arouse interest in pollution control. Much work has been carried out in collaboration with officials of the Ontario Water Resources Commission, which is responsible for pollution control in the province.

7

Providing for Recreation

Recreation was not mentioned in the Conservation Authorities Act when it was passed in 1946. However, in most of the conservation reports prepared by the Conservation Branch, commencing with the first for the upper Thames in 1945, much space was given to the need of recreation and in all cases areas were recommended for this purpose.

The first opportunity for including recreation on a large scale in a conservation project presented itself in connection with the lands abutting the Fanshawe Dam and reservoir on the Thames River. Up to this time engineers closely followed the orthodox method of controlling flood waters by constructing dams which served a dual purpose of holding back floods and providing supplementary summer flow in the downstream channels of the rivers. The Shand Dam and later, the Conestoga, both on the Grand River, are of this type and while the fringe lands of these reservoirs have been developed for recreation, it is recognized that summer-flow reservoirs, which of necessity must be drawn down during the summer months (leaving unsightly shorelines), can provide only second-class recreation areas.

When the Fanshawe on the Thames was first planned it seemed natural to follow the orthodox design of the Shand Dam and reservoir. However, on further consideration, realizing that inland lakes in Southwestern Ontario were few in number, the planners decided to provide for a permanent lake approximately one-half mile wide by four miles in length. This was the method used on some of the reservoirs of the Muskingum Watershed Conservancy district in Ohio, where such lakes have become popular. The building of Fanshawe Lake as a recreational centre meant that 10,000 acre-feet of flood storage would have to be sacrificed, and be provided for in the other reservoirs planned for upstream development. But this was considered worthwhile when it was foreseen that such a lake would form the focal point of an extensive park. The upper Thames report of 1945 dealt in detail with this new concept, and by using the fringe lands of the reservoir, a park area extending several miles up the valley was made available.

To assist in this project the Authority appointed a parks and recreation advisory

Richardson beach is a favourite gathering spot in the J. Cameron Wilson park on the shores of Fanshawe Lake, north and east of London.

board with Dr E.G. Pleva, head of the department of geography, University of Western Ontario, as chairman, with prominent officials and others interested in conservation as members. This brought the community into the early stages of the planning so that the residents could feel they were a part of the undertaking. In addition, Dr Pleva arranged that two of his students would assist in the planning, with the result that Malcolm Murray wrote his master's thesis on the recreational potential of the valley and Alan Connor produced a present and recommended land-use plan for the land adjacent to the proposed reservoir. The work of the board and the field studies of the two students provided the basic data for completing the plans of the proposed park.

Another authority which at this time foresaw the possibilities of recreation as a part of the flood-control scheme was the Ausable, when it built the channel in the vicinity of Port Franks to carry heavy flows from the main river and to ameliorate flooding in the village. Here again, adopting a method used on the Muskingum, a buffer strip 600 feet wide was purchased on each side of the channel and this, through the years, has been developed as a recreation area, including a lucrative summer cottage development.

However, if recreation was to find its rightful place in the conservation programme, it could not be limited to fringe lands of flood-control schemes. The authors of the conservation reports envisioned a type of property independent of flood-control lands, property described as a 'multi-purpose conservation area.' This included flood-plain lands, river-valley slopes, woodlots, reforestation, demonstration of improved farming principles, wildlife habitat, swamps which are the source of streams, and recreation areas.

Hunters practise marksmanship at the Cold Creek conservation area. At least one authority has constructed duck blinds and operates a controlled hunting pro-gramme during the season.

In the autumn of 1948 the Humber valley authority proposed a scheme which would include a number of conservation projects in one contiguous area, would captivate the imagination of the member municipalities and give them something on which to concentrate their efforts. This resulted in a multi-purpose scheme as described in the conservation reports. Accordingly, H.F. Crown of the staff of the Conservation Branch, with the assistance of R.D. Hodges, who at that time was consultant to the Humber authority, selected an area in King Township, two miles northeast of Bolton, and prepared a brief to the Ontario government requesting approval of the scheme and financial assistance to carry it out.

The brief was presented to the ministers concerned and, after some delay, persistent prodding, further consultations and correspondence, the scheme was rejected. This decision loosed a storm of protest from the three Toronto dailies, which were unanimous in their criticism of the government for rejecting an excel-lent conservation project. From the newspaper clippings which have been pre-served – and there must have been more – there are 168 inches of single-column type and 29 inches of editorial material, or, in all, more than one full page of newspaper space given to the controversy.

Today, a member of a conservation authority could read the Humber brief and be puzzled why this first multi-purpose scheme was rejected; by present standards it is almost-perfect in its proposition. Why was it turned down by the government?

First, the act establishing the conservation authorities made no mention of land acquisition for recreational purposes. In the minds of most people the authorities were in business to prevent future floods, not to provide recreational facilities. Second, the brief's title – 'Humber Conservation Park' – was ill chosen; the association of the word 'park' with conservation did not ring true. Finally, in 1949 the creation of recreational facilities did not have the same appeal it does today; in 1949 there were only eight provincial parks in Ontario; in 1970 there were one hundred.

(After the Metropolitan Toronto and Region Conservation Authority had been formed, it acquired the same land with government assistance and the Cold Creek conservation area was officially opened by the Honourable J.W. Spooner in 1962.)

On 20 January 1953 the Honourable W.K. Warrender was appointed minister of planning and development. It is an accepted procedure with senior civil servants that the appointment of a new minister is a propitious time to present again schemes and ideas which were not acceptable to the former incumbent. Accordingly, and remembering that there had been a dramatic change in thinking in the preceding four years with respect to recreation, it was suggested to Werden Leavens, who was chairman of the Humber authority, that he try again for a multi-purpose conservation scheme. As the former site was not available the authority engaged Gordon Culham, a well-known park planner, to investigate and recommend another area. The lands selected this time were in Albion Township, traversed by the main branch of the Humber River and Centreville Creek and covering approximately 160 acres. The question of a name came up. Remembering the objection to 'Humber Conservation *Park*' in the former brief, we searched about for a more appropriate title which would cover any type of conservation endeavour. Finally, because of the rolling countryside which characterized this part of Albion, it was appropriately named the 'Albion Hills conservation area.' In this way the term 'conservation area' came into being and has continued to be used for projects of this kind through the years.

When Mr Warrender met the Humber delegation, much to their surprise and delight he was not only in accord with the proposed scheme and encouraged them to purchase the block of land, but, in addition, urged the authority to buy more land before costs became excessive.

After this fruitful meeting with the minister, it was evident that if the authorities were to be permitted to use land for recreation, the Conservation Authorities Act must be amended. At the 1954 session of the legislature, Mr Warrender was instrumental in amending the act:

Section 17 for the purpose of carrying out a scheme, an authority has power,
i/ to acquire lands, with the approval of the minister and to use lands acquired in connection with a scheme, for recreational purposes, and to erect, or permit to be erected, buildings, booths and facilities for such purposes and to make charges for admission thereto and use thereof.

It will be noticed that the wording 'recreational purposes' is subsidiary to 'lands acquired in connection with a scheme.' In other words, lands could not be acquired solely for the purposes of establishing a recreation area, but must be included in lands which are acquired for conservation purposes. Or as an editorial in the Toronto *Globe and Mail* put it: 'Conservation is the supreme objective; a conservation project will yield parks, but parks do not constitute a conservation programme.'

It was abundantly evident that the winds of popular opinion and governmental sanction had begun to swing behind recreation. As already noted, recreational parks in Ontario were in short supply. From 1954, when the act was amended, until 1970, the conservation authorities alone created 293 conservation areas which, added to fringe lands around reservoirs, brought the total recreational space to 87,340 acres.

There is no set of absolute standards against which a potential conservation area is compared. It must, of course be a property which will contribute to and derive benefit from a large, integrated conservation project. The following tables group all conservation areas by type:

NATURAL LAKES

As the presence of water adds greatly to the use of a recreation area, it is not surprising that the authorities acquired natural lakes whenever possible. Most of these have wooded areas and ample open spaces for recreational activities. Besides the usual aquatic sports which are popular on such lakes, some have had undesirable fish removed and have been restocked with more desirable species.

CONSERVATION AUTHORITY	CONSERVATION AREA
Cataraqui	Gould
Crowe	Paudash
Grand	Pinehurst
	Puslinch
Halton	Crawford's
Junction Creek	Laurentian
	Minnow
	Ramsay
Lakehead	Hazelwood
MTRCA	Heart
	St George
Napanee	Second Depot
Otonabee	Chemong
Rideau	Foley
	Mill Pond
	Portland Bay
Sauble	Charles
	McNab
	Shallow
Saugeen	Schmidt
Sydenham	Campbell
	Coldstream
	Warwick
Whitson	Whitson

FRINGE LANDS OF RESERVOIRS

In addition to the natural lakes, the man-made lakes formed by the many reservoirs large and small, with their extensive fringe lands, add an additional 25,000 acres to the total of conservation areas.

CONSERVATION AUTHORITY	CONSERVATION AREA
Ausable	Morrison Dam
	Parkhill
Big Creek	Deer Creek
	Hay Creek
	Lehman Dam
	Norwich Dam
	Quance Dam
	Teeterville Dam
Cataraqui	Buell's Creek
	Little Cataraqui
Credit	Monora
	Orangeville
	Terra Cotta
Grand	Belwood Lake
	Blenheim Bends
	Canagagigue
	Conestoga Lake
	Everton
	Guelph
	Montrose
	Shades Mill
Halton	Scotch Block
Hamilton	Christie
	Red Hill Creek
Holland	Rogers
Junction Creek	Maley
	Nickeldale
Lower Thames	Sharon Creek
Maitland	Brussels
	Galbraith
	Gorrie
MTRCA	Albion Hills
	Bolton Dam
	Boyd
	Claireville
	Ebenezer
	Nashville
Moira	Deerock Dam
	Deloro
Niagara	Binbrook
	Chippawa Creek
	Virgil
North Grey	Clendinning-Haines
Nottawasaga	New Lowell
	Tottenham
	Utopia

CONSERVATION AUTHORITY	CONSERVATION AREA
Upper Thames	Dorchester
	Fanshawe Park
	Pittock
	Wildwood

BEACHES

Small beaches on the Great Lakes, accessible to the public, are not very plentiful; consequently where the watershed under the jurisdiction of an authority includes such desirable features they have been included in a conservation area.

CONSERVATION AUTHORITY	CONSERVATION AREA
Big Creek	Norfolk County
Hamilton	Fifty-Mile Point
Lakehead	Hurkett Cove
MTRCA	Duffins Creek
	Lower Rouge
Niagara	Long Beach
North Grey	Ainlie Woods
Prince Edward	Mississauga
Sauble	Arran Lake
Saugeen	Brucedale
Sydenham	Crothers

RIVERS, STREAMS AND CREEKS

This group of recreation areas is large and many areas deserve mentioning in detail. However space permits the describing of only one. All will agree that this is the most spectacular acquisition by an authority where a large river is involved.

CONSERVATION AUTHORITY	CONSERVATION AREA
Ausable	Port Franks
	Rock Glen
	Thedford
Big Creek	Black Creek
	Cornell
	Port Burwell
	Rowan Mills
	Waterford
Catfish	Springwater
Central Lake Ontario	Enniskillen
	Harmony Valley
	Heber Down
Credit	Meadowvale
Crowe	Crowebridge
Ganaraska	Coburg
	Port Hope
	Silver Glen

CONSERVATION AUTHORITY	CONSERVATION AREA
Grand	Brant
	Elora Bissell
	Elora Gorge (see below)
	Grand Valley
	Rockwood
Halton	Wilcox
Hamilton	Redhill Creek
Holland	Holland Landing
	Thornton Bales
	Wesley Brooks
	Whitchurch
Lakehead	Cascades
	Wishart
Lower Thames	Millstream
Maitland	Ethel
	Falls Reserve
MTRCA	Cold Creek
	Frenchmans Bay
	Greenwood
	Humber Trails
	King Creek
	Petticoat Creek
Moira	Plainfield
	Price
	Vanderwater
Niagara	Balls Falls
	Beamer Memorial
	Stevensville
North Grey	Eugenia Falls
	Pottawatomi
	Rocklyn Creek
Otonabee	Warsaw Caves
Rideau	Baxter
Sauble	Indian Falls
	Oxenden Creek
Saugeen	Durham
	Southampton
Upper Thames	Dingmans Creek
	Reynolds Creek

The gorge of the Grand River at Elora is a unique scenic attraction which cannot be duplicated in Southern Ontario and is only surpassed in grandeur by the mighty Niagara chasm. Here the historic and picturesque Grand River tumbles over fifty-foot falls and winds its way for a tortuous mile and one-half between sheer walls of limestone towering seventy-five to one hundred feet above the bed of the stream. This is the most spectacular stretch of the Grand River.

For many years the scenic attraction of the gorge has been admired by countless visitors from far and near including geologists, photographers and artists. An

The Elora gorge, spectacular scenery along the Grand River Conservation Authority watershed.

interesting painting of the entrance to the gorge hangs in Trinity College, Toronto, painted by Arthur Cox in 1871 entitled 'The Silurian Gates.' Silurian, in geological time, is a period of the Paleozoic era, 360 million years ago, when air-breathing animals and land plants first appeared on the earth.

The 328 acres in this area, owned by the Grand authority, includes the gorge, and the flat land above and adjacent to it, on both sides of the river. Much of this has been developed as a well-planned park with many amenities; the remainder is used for demonstration including reforestation and land-use practices.

For leadership in acquiring this beautiful property by the authority, grateful credit is given to Mrs K. Marsdon who for many years chaired the parks and recreation advisory board of the authority.

SWAMPS, BOGS AND MARSHES

Swamps, bogs and marshes have been acquired, not only because they are nature's reservoirs and feed the headwaters of streams, but also for their botanical interest.

The Byron bog is a unique 57-acre boreal bog with sixty feet of sphagnum and many other bog plants including orchids. It is a relic of the glacial age within the environs of the city of London and is used as an outdoor laboratory by students of the University of Western Ontario.

CONSERVATION AUTHORITY	CONSERVATION AREA
Central Lake Ontario	Cranberry marsh
Grand	Luther marsh
Hamilton	Beverly swamp
	Summit bog
Maitland	Saratoga swamp
Niagara	Willoughby marsh
Nottawasaga	Osprey wetland
Otonabee	Cavan swamp
Upper Thames	Byron bog

ISLANDS

One of the island areas, Byng Island, situated near the mouth of the Grand River, is partly wooded and has been developed into a 187-acre recreation area with many interesting features. The other two, Beament Island and Kolfage Island, are offshore in Lake Huron. They were acquired by the Sauble Valley Conservation Authority in 1970 and 1969 respectively and have been left in their natural state.

CONSERVATION AUTHORITY	CONSERVATION AREA
Grand	Byng Island
Sauble	Beament Island
	Kolfage Island

OBSERVATION AND STUDY

An interesting group of properties have been acquired and left in their natural state – little wilderness pockets – for observation and study. Included in this group are the wildlife sanctuaries which, thanks to the generosity of their former owners, have been deeded to the authorities.

CONSERVATION AUTHORITY	CONSERVATION AREA
Big Creek	Fisher
	Oatman
	Port Royal
	Sutton Pond
	Vanessa
Credit	Hillsburgh Farm
Grand	Bannister-Wrigley
	F.W.R. Dickson
	Hanlon
	Laurel Creek
	Oneida
	Taquanyak
	Victoria Mills
Halton	Burns Nature Area
	Mountsburg
Hamilton	Spencer Gorge
MTRCA	Glen Haffy
Napanee	Arden
Niagara	St Johns

White's pond, a placid spot for a rest on a hiking trip to White's bush in the Springwater conservation area.

CONSERVATION AUTHORITY	CONSERVATION AREA
North Grey	Bognor
	Peasmarsh
Otonabee	Beaver Meadow
	Heber Rogers
	Miller Creek
	Squirrel Creek
	Stewarts Woods
Sauble	Rankin River
	Sucker Creek
	Walker Woods
Saugeen	Headquarters

OLD MILLS

These are areas which have as their dominant feature an old mill with enough land to qualify as a conservation area – the largest is 271 acres. Also included in this group are the Black Creek conservation area and the Doon conservation area, on which two pioneer villages of the same names have been developed.

Inglis Falls, a delightful cascade where the Pottawatami River tumbles over the Niagara escarpment, has been preserved by the North Grey Conservation Authority.

CONSERVATION AUTHORITY	CONSERVATION AREA
Big Creek	Backus
	Vienna
Credit	Limehouse
	Old School House
Ganaraska	Balls Mill
Grand	Doon Pioneer Village
Lakehead	Granite Point
Lower Thames	Lighthouse
MTRCA	Black Creek Roblin Mill
	Bruce's Mill
	McMichael
Moira	O'Hara Mill
North Grey	Inglis Falls
	Owen Sound Mill Dam
Nottawasaga	Carruthers
Otonabee	Hope Dam Mill
	Lang Mill

SMALL COMMUNITY AREAS

These recreational areas have been planned, for the most part, for family picnics. Some are located within the environs of a village or town. A few have been located around the site of an old mill and in some instances the mill pond has been rebuilt. Others are old picnic sites which have been used for many years by the local folk and now under the supervision of the authority are properly managed and maintained. These areas are the ones best known perhaps by the children of the authorities; though small, they contribute to healthy outdoor fun for many thousands.

CONSERVATION AUTHORITY	CONSERVATION AREA
Ausable	Exeter
	Lucan
Big Creek	Abigail Becker
	Brook
Ganaraska	Garden Hill
Grand	Bresleau
	Caledonia
	Drayton Valley
	W.C. Scott
	Silver Creek
	Stanley Park
Halton	Campbellville
Holland	Mabel Davis
Junction Creek	Garson
Kettle Creek	Belmont
Lower Thames	Delaware
	Harwich
	Longwood
Lower Trent	Glen Miller
	Kings Mill
	Sager – Oak Hills
Maitland	Harrison – Minto
	Pioneer
	Sunshine
	Wroxeter
MTRCA	Bolton
	Claremont
	Milne
	Stouffville
	Uxbridge
Moira	Flinton
Napanee	Forest Mills
	Newburgh
	Portland
North Grey	Flesherton
	Meaford
Otonabee	N. Monaghan
Prince Edward	Macauley Mountain
Sauble	Tara
Saugeen	Allan Park
	Lockerby Mill
	Markdale
	Mildmay – Carrick
	Varney
Sault Ste Marie	Fort Creek

CONSERVATION AUTHORITY	CONSERVATION AREA
Sydenham Valley	Petrolia
	Strathroy
Upper Thames	Centreville
	Embro
	Fullarton
	Harrington
	Kirkton
	Shakespeare
	Westminster

THE NIAGARA ESCARPMENT

One of the outstanding physiographic features of Southern Ontario is the Niagara escarpment. This limestone formation, revealed as sheer cliffs in some areas and gently rolling hills in others, traverses the southern part of the province in a sinuous line from Niagara Falls north to Tobermory at the tip of the Bruce Peninsula. The eight conservation authorities through which it passes have all played active roles in the preservation and control of lands on the escarpment.

During the early years, while authority programmes were not designed so much to acquire escarpment lands *per se*, reforestation, water-control and recreation projects were undertaken along it as a part of the authorities' total watershed programme. Early acquisitions included Kelso, Esquesing and Mount Nemo conservation areas, secured during 1958 and 1959 by the Halton Conservation Authority. Albion Hills conservation area and Glen Haffy conservation area were acquired by the Metropolitan Toronto and Region Conservation Authority in 1955 and 1959 respectively. Numerous key areas were purchased by the Sauble and North Grey Conservation Authorities largely through the efforts of Mac Kirk, the resources manager. By 1967, the eight conservation authorities had acquired some 6,000 acres of escarpment lands.

In March 1967, in response to public concern over the future of the escarpment, then Premier John Robarts announced a 'wide-ranging study of the Niagara escarpment with a view to preserving its entire length from Queenston to Tobermory and Manitoulin Island as a recreation area for the people of Ontario.' Professor L.O. Gertler directed the study and it was presented to the public in October 1969.

A direct result of its recommendations was the decision to allow conservation authorities a subsidy of 75 percent of the cost of escarpment land acquisition. This meant that for every dollar raised by an authority to purchase land in the escarpment, the provincial government would add three dollars. There followed a rapid increase in land acquisition, such that by 1970 close to 11,000 acres of escarpment land were owned by conservation authorities for public enjoyment.

CONSERVATION AUTHORITY	CONSERVATION AREA
Credit	Belfountain
	Silver Creek
Halton	Escarpment
	Esquesing
	Hilton Falls
	Mount Nemo
	Sixteen Valley

The Gertler report on the resources of the Niagara escarpment recommended that the province buy the Forks of the Credit, a particularly handsome region of the uplands, and create parkland.

CONSERVATION AUTHORITY	CONSERVATION AREA
Hamilton	Crooks Hollow
	Devils Punch Bowl
	Dundas Valley
	Fifty-Mile Point
	Hopkins
	Tiffany Falls
Nottawasaga	Escarpment
Sauble	Bruces Caves
	Osler Bluffs
	Keppel Escarpment
	Skinner Bluffs
	Spirit Rock
MTRCA	Glen Haffy
	Albion Hills
Niagara	Balls Falls
North Grey	Inglis Falls
	Jones Falls

FLOOD PLAINS

The programme of flood-plain mapping and acquisition was initiated following the disastrous Hurricane Hazel flood of 15 October 1954 and continued as a major and top-priority programme of the authorities over the years. Initially the programme was limited to those authorities with existing flood problems in large urban centres. In later years, however, the more rural authorities became active in this field to prevent the indiscriminate development of lands subject to flooding and thus eliminate the risk of further flood damages and possible loss of life. While the main activity was centred around the Metropolitan Toronto area, the Upper and Lower Thames, Kettle Creek, Grand, Holland, Central Lake Ontario, Junction Creek, Lakehead and Sault Ste Marie Conservation Authorities also had programmes under way. Approximately 89,100 acres of land have been acquired and developed for recreation and other compatible uses or left in their natural states as open space areas, as of December 1970.

CONSERVATION AUTHORITY	CONSERVATION AREA
Grand	Brantford-Paris
	Kitchener
	Silver Creek
Halton	Oakville – Sixteen-Mile Creek
Lower Thames	Big Bend
MTRCA	Frenchmans Bay
	Woodbridge
Napanee	Napanee
Otonabee	Brooks Marble

WOODLAND

Such areas for the most part are small stands of mature timber, not included in the authority forest, and purchased more for their aesthetic interest than for the wood products they will yield.

CONSERVATION AUTHORITY	CONSERVATION AREA
Maitland	Sunshine (Morris)
MTRCA	Glen Major
	Goodwood
	Palgrave
Niagara	Comfort Maple Tree
Nottawasaga	Tiffin
Saugeen	Mount Forest (Angus Smith)
Upper Thames	Dr Murray Forest

BOAT LAUNCHING SITES

In all areas where facilities are available and boating is permitted, the necessary launching and landing sites are built. However, there are a few such launching sites, which because of their importance, are included in a special group.

CONSERVATION AUTHORITY	CONSERVATION AREA
Cataraqui	Charleston Lake
	Cronk Lake
	Hay Bay
	Loughborough Lake
	Mosquito Lake
	Sydenham Lake
	Seeleys Bay
Lower Thames	Cornhill (Thames Grove)
Otonabee	Youngs Point
	Indian River Canoe Trail

SKIING, WINTER ACTIVITIES

Three authorities, the Grand, Halton and Metropolitan Toronto and Region Conservation Authorities, have developed skiing facilities which are self-supporting in those areas where fees are charged. In 1963–4 the Grand River Conservation Authority acquired the Chicopee Hills which provides tobogganing and skiing with a chairlift, chalet, two T-bar tows and a beginners' tow. The Halton Region Conservation Authority acquired the assets of a private operation in 1966 at the Kelso conservation area, which included two T-bars, a rope tow, chalet and snowmaking equipment. The Metropolitan Toronto and Region Conservation Authority provides two ski tows at the Albion Hills conservation area and a beginners' tow in the Boyd conservation area.

CONSERVATION AUTHORITY	CONSERVATION AREA
Grand	Chicopee
Halton	Kelso
Prince Edward	McAuley Mountain
MTRCA	Albion Hills
	Boyd

LOOKOUTS

Last but very important are areas an acre or more in size, some of which are included in large conservation areas, where the traveller can turn off the highway and view a vista of superb Ontario landscape, which, considering the expanding meaning of the definition today, can be considered conservation of the spirit.

CONSERVATION AUTHORITY	CONSERVATION AREA
Central Lake Ontario	Long Sault
Ganaraska	Richardson
Lower Trent	Proctor Park
North Grey	East Rocks
	Epping
	Old Baldy
Prince Edward	Dug Hill
Sauble	Colpoy Range

Most of the properties acquired for conservation authority recreational use have continued to be known by their local names. What a rich heritage of the Anglo-Saxon tongue, salted here and there with additions from French and Indian Languages: Enniskillen, Limehouse, Sylvan Glen, Blenheim Bends, Cascades, Vanderwater, Warsaw Caves, Dingle, Pottawatomi, Utopia, Belfountain, Terra Cotta, Deer Rock, Virgil, Paudash Lake, Granite Point, Peasmarsh, Beautiful Joe, Esquesing, Mount Nemo, Rattlesnake Point, Crooks Hollow, Devils Punchbowl, Tiffany Falls, Slough of Despond, Spirit Rock, Taquanyah, Dug Hill, Silver Creek, Petticoat, Harmony, Shakespeare, Mosquito Lake, Chicopee Hills and the most euphonious, Balls Falls.

The Glen Haffy lookout provides a panoramic view of the Humber valley lying below the Niagara escarpment in the MTRCA watershed.

A study of the tabular matter above will make it clear that not all conservation areas have parks; some, such as swamps, wilderness areas, and wildlife sanctuaries are used for study and observation. Also in most areas, and especially the large ones, only a part is developed for intensive recreation, the remainder being used for the primary purpose of a conservation area – woodlot management, reforestation, demonstrations of soil and water conservation. But even these 'study areas,' however, are available for wider activities such as nature hiking and bird watching.

The types of park facilities provided for public use depend on the natural features of the area, those with bodies of water being the most popular. In the description of facilities which follows, only a few areas have a full complement of facilities; the emphasis in all parks is on what is sometimes referred to as 'passive recreation,' in contrast to organized sport and fairground amusements.

The park facilities developed in conservation areas, include family and group picnic sites, overnight camping, cottage sites, swimming, fishing, boating including sail, and other aquatic recreation.

In some areas, power boats are not permitted. Hiking is popular and some of the trails ramble along for five miles. One very popular area has a fishing pond reserved for children; it's a favourite of young people. One area has facilities which provide practice and competition areas for small arms, target and field archery, dog trials and fly-casting. Also a special feature at this same area is the hunter-safety training courses which are conducted there.

In recent years, several areas have been open for winter use including skating, skiing, tobogganning; in some areas snowmobiles are permitted. Some authorities specialize in old-time, horse-drawn, sleigh rides and for those who are warm-blooded, family picnics, overnight camping and hiking facilities are provided.

A spring outing which has become very popular in recent years is a visit to a maple syrup shanty located in the maple bush of conservation areas. Here, the old and new methods of reducing maple sap to syrup and sugar are demonstrated and these products, fortified with pancakes, are for sale. Four authorities – the Halton region, the Metropolitan Toronto region, the Moira and the Otonabee – hold maple syrup demonstrations in the bush each spring. Literally tens of thousands of children and adults – about 100,000 in 1970 – flock each year to these demonstrations, which are the first large event in the conservation authorities' programme after the long Ontario winter.

Four conservation authorities provide sugaring-off parties in their forests. This one is in the Metro Toronto region.

Included in the conservation areas listed above is a group which deserves special mention. These are ones which, because of the magnanimity of the original owners, have been deeded to the conservation authorities for long-time use.

METROPOLITAN TORONTO AND REGION CONSERVATION AUTHORITY

McMichael conservation area and McMichael conservation collection of art
In 1965, Mr and Mrs Robert McMichael gave the people of Canada their magnificent collection of Canadian paintings and their lodge-size, log cabin home on a ridge overlooking the Humber River valley near Kleinburg, Ontario. An added feature of the McMichael conservation area is the Tom Thomson shack (moved from the Rosedale ravine, Toronto) in which he did some of his paintings. It still contains the artist's paraphernalia.

J. Grant Glassco conservation area
In 1936, J. Grant Glassco, a financier living in Toronto, became enamoured with the attractive countryside of the Humber River valley and purchased 150 acres which he named Cold Creek Farm. During ensuing years, he increased the size of his property to 580 acres. His will donated 480 acres of his holdings to the Ontario Heritage Foundation for the use of the people of Ontario and as a memorial to his family.

As the Glassco property is adjacent to the McMichael and the Boyd areas, it seemed appropriate to the foundation that it should be developed and managed by the authority. Accordingly, under an agreement between the foundation, Mrs Willa Glassco, widow of the donor, and the Metropolitan Toronto and Region Conservation Authority, the authority was granted the right of possession for a period of twenty-five years renewable, provided that the authority agree to develop, maintain and administer the area to the same standards and for the same general purposes as its other conservation areas, subject to the approval of the foundation.

The three conservation areas – the McMichael, the Boyd and the Glassco – are contiguous, totalling approximately 2,000 acres. In sum, these three areas stretch three and one-half miles along the Humber valley, conservation-land for all time to come.

HOLLAND VALLEY CONSERVATION AUTHORITY

Thornton Bales conservation area
Thornton Bales conservation area is located in King Township and is named as a memorial to the donor (1871–1967) who was intensely interested in the welfare of the people in his own neighbourhood and beyond. In later years his interest included conservation and, as a practical demonstration, he deeded fifty acres of bush to the township. When the authority commenced expanding its programme, the township, in its wisdom, transferred the property to the authority for management and preservation.

Mabel Davis conservation area
This property is named in honour of Mabel Davis, a sister of Aubrey Davis, who sponsored the King Township survey in 1938, and a member of an old respected family in Newmarket, in appreciation for deeding to the authority a property of seventeen acres which she had developed as a bird sanctuary. It is situated adjacent to Bayview Avenue, north of Davis Drive with the Holland River forming its west boundary.

Whitchurch conservation area
This area comprising twenty-five acres on the fifth concession of Whitchurch Township is one of the many activities initiated by the Whitchurch Conservation Club. Until 1956 it was under the supervision of this group, when it was sold to the township for one dollar, on the understanding that it be transferred to the Holland Valley Conservation Authority as a conservation area.

SAUGEEN VALLEY CONSERVATION AUTHORITY

Durham conservation area
In 1962, A.J. Metzer, a merchant in Hanover and an ardent conservationist, donated 35 acres of land to the authority for a conservation area. With this as a core, the authority increased the area to 185 acres and named it the Durham conservation area. The land borders on the Saugeen River in the town of Durham and includes a reservoir formed by a new dam built by the Ontario Department of Public Works and named for the donor. This spacious conservation area within the boundaries of the town provides a variety of recreational facilities including acquatic activities.

OTONABEE REGION CONSERVATION AUTHORITY

Heber Rogers wildlife sanctuary
This 90 acre, wooded, wildlife sanctuary, a gift to the Otonabee authority, is

situated in Smith township in Peterborough County near Clear Lake in the Kawarthas. The wooden sign with incised lettering was unveiled on 16 July 1966 and bears the inscription:

'Heber Rogers Wildlife Sanctuary – In memory of Heber Symonds Rogers, 1896–1958, a veteran of World Wars I and II, a man of broad human sympathies, expert in woodcrafts and water skills (son of R.B. Rogers, designer of the Peterborough liftlocks), husband of Rosamond Rogers who has donated this sanctuary as a memorial to one who, as a man and a boy loved these Kawartha woods and waters.'

Early in the 1940s, the first rumblings were heard of what might be called the battle to save the flood-plain lands and valley slopes in Southern Ontario. These lands are often associated only with problems of flood control, and, in truth, they are an important part of such problems. On the other hand, their potential for recreation is almost unlimited.

When the Conservation Branch commenced the river valley surveys, it soon became evident how much flood damage was caused by the foolish encroachments of man-made structures in the river valleys. In the early reports this problem was emphasized strongly and the necessity of correcting this unwise practice was mentioned time and time again. The most critical statement regarding this problem appeared in the upper Thames report:

When we are honest with ourselves and get down to the bottom of the flood problem, about ninety percent of the flood damage is a result of man's damn foolishness in building his roads, railroads, factories, houses, farms and what not on land which plainly belongs to the river. When he built there, the evidence that the river had used that land for flood purposes was plainly visible, and when that evidence is there you can be darn sure the river will again flood those lands. It would be much simpler and more economical to retire them from human occupancy ... and give them back to the river for flood purposes.

Toronto was among the first to recognize the value of preserving these areas on a large scale and many militant voices were raised to preserve and protect the valleys of the rivers which drained an area of approximately one thousand square miles into Lake Ontario through the Toronto region.

On November 1946, F.G. Gardiner, QC, vice-chairman of the Toronto Planning Board who was also associated with the Toronto and Suburban Planning Board, presented a paper on regional planning at the convention on conservation in South-central Ontario sponsored by the Conservation Branch in Toronto. In his address he stated: 'When the planning act was passed in 1946 it gave power to the minister of the Department of Planning and Development to approve a planning authority for the whole or any part of a municipality or for one or more municipalities.' At the request of the municipalities concerned, the minister established a regional planning area representing Toronto and the twelve smaller municipalities adjacent to the city. 'The duties of the planning authority,' Mr Gardiner went on to say, 'are to prepare a plan indicating land uses, that is, which part of the area shall be designated for agricultural purposes, which part shall be designated as industrial areas, which part should be commercial areas and which part designated as residential area. Further, [the authority] is also to consider the broad question of transportation. It shall also consider and recommend with respect to a programme of sanitation, and also with respect to the establishment of green belts and parks.' This plan when approved by the minister became the region's 'official plan.'

The pertinent part of the plan with respect to this narrative is the establishment of green belts and parks. In a report released by the Toronto Suburban Planning Board about this time, a map was included showing proposed outer and inner green belts for the region. The outer green belt commenced at Hamilton and extended northeast to a point about thirty miles north of Toronto, thence curving southeast to Oshawa. The inner green belt commenced at the mouth of the Humber River and followed the valley north to its headwaters, then crossed over and returned to the lake following the Don valley and the valleys of the small rivers to the east.

At the time the report was released, the outer green belt was considered by many as an extraordinary exercise in wishful thinking, but, with the acquisition of land in this area by authorities, and with regional planning inaugurated by the provincial government, the possibility of such an outer green belt is beginning to come into focus.

The inner green belt, on the other hand, was decidedly realistic and with the acquisition of much of the valley land by the Metropolitan Toronto and Region Conservation Authority in the area under its supervision, is rapidly becoming a reality.

Once the official plan was approved there was no problem regarding the use of land designated for agriculture, industry and residential: these parcels of land could be developed by private enterprise. But the land in the valleys was a different problem. Much of the valley land was privately owned and was regulated by the planning act which required that all new subdivisions be approved by the minister of planning and development; for obvious reasons the department would not approve flood-plain land or valley slopes for *any* use other than recreation. This posed a dilemma with respect to the status of these lands as it was reasonable to assume that they could not be frozen indefinitely at the expense of the owner. The only alternative was for the municipalities concerned to purchase suitable areas as funds would permit. To attempt to buy *all* the valley land which should be reserved for recreation was considered impossible without government assistance.

While the battle to preserve the valley lands of the Toronto region was in progress, one volunteer group made a valuable impact on the thinking of the people in this area. The Don Valley Conservation Association was organized by Roy Cadwell, Charles Sauriol and Ran Freeland in November 1946 with the slogan: 'Conservation, restoration, beautification and recreation.' Later, when Roy Cadwell retired, Charles Sauriol became the guiding force and spearheaded a vigorous programme of public relations, which among other results, brought about the formation of the Don Valley Conservation Authority in April 1948. A noteworthy contribution to this program by Charlie Sauriol was the publishing of a quarterly magazine, *The Cardinal*, which stressed the long and interesting history of the Don

Weston, Raymore Drive, 15 October 1954. Hurricane Hazel whipped the Humber River into a maelstrom of destruction inundating these homes on the river's flood plains and, in this area alone, causing thirty-eight deaths. This scene of desolation has now been transformed into a peaceful park.

valley and the necessity of preserving it for future generations. This magazine, which was published from 1951 to 1956, was a labour of love on the part of the editor, who wrote most of the copy and was responsible for the financing of the publication.

During these years the four authorities – Etobicoke-Mimico; Humber; Don; and Rouge, Duffin, Highland and Petticoat – were established and each joined the battle to preserve the valleys in its watershed.

Victory, however, was not yet in sight. Even Charlie Sauriol, who is noted for his contagious exuberance where matters of conservation are concerned, published a gloomy prophecy in *The Cardinal*: 'Perhaps, in a century hence, the thing we will most regret is the destruction of Toronto's one-time magnificent ravine system.'

It has already been noted that Hurricane Hazel struck Ontario 15–16 October 1954, and that one of the aftermaths was the splendid work of the Flood Homes and Buildings Assistance Board which established the policy that the acquisition of flood-plain land is an integral part of a flood-control project. As a result, conservation authorities undertook surveys of their valley lands – in some cases called open-spaces surveys – and began planning for their use. In the Metropolitan Toronto and Region Conservation Authority there was an upsurge in interest in this forward step. Municipalities which had acquired such lands, following the hurricane or before, transferred them or sold them for a nominal amount to the authority for development as parks.

Where such lands were situated within the municipality of Metropolitan Toronto, an agreement was made between the authority and the municipality which permits the lands to be developed, financed and managed for park purposes by the Metropolitan Parks Board. For some years this development had been proceeding apace on lands within Metro and also those which the authority has acquired outside Metro. It is anticipated that in the near future there will be several miles of river-valley parks, approximately 7,200 acres, developed under this excellent scheme.

8
Surrounded by the Past

Verschoyle Benson Blake, the historian, has written:

We need something more than archives to tell us how our forefathers lived. To know this, we must preserve buildings, furniture and tools. We must know how these things were made and the way they were, and the uses for which they were intended. To read this in books and pictures is a good thing, but it is infinitely better to preserve some of the things themselves. To let these be lost through our indifference is to deprive future generations of a heritage to which they are entitled.

Conservation reports, with their heavy burden of technical material, can be uninteresting and sometimes positively dull to laymen. Realizing this, and remembering that it would be laymen who would be most involved in carrying out a municipally oriented programme of conservation if the recommendations of the Ganaraska report were implemented, its authors decided that to make the report more interesting the first chapter would deal with the historical background of the area. In other words, the introductory historical section would be the sugar-coated pill, which, it was hoped, would stimulate the interest of the reader and entice him to read the report in full.

Although the small Ganaraska watershed with its rolling topography, extremes of soils, a river which floods periodically, and its former abundance of forest products was ideally suited for the survey, it was equally rich in historical interest extending back for 150 years. The settlement at the mouth of the Ganaraska River, known first as Smith's Creek, for a short time as Toronto, and later as Port Hope, had its beginning in the 1790s, at the same time as Lieutenant-Governor Simcoe was establishing the town of York, now Toronto, some fifty miles to the west.

When it was decided to print the Ganaraska report, a meeting was called in Toronto of those responsible for the promotion of the survey to decide the general format and to discuss abridgements or additions. Most of the members of the Ontario Interdepartmental Committee on Conservation and Rehabilitation were present, as well as a small group from the Advisory Committee of Reconstruction, including Dr Leonard Marsh who was my opposite in Ottawa. Dr R.C. Wallace, principal and vice-chancellor of Queen's University and chairman of the sub-committee on conservation and development of natural resources of the Advisory Committee of Reconstruction, was in the chair.

After some discussion on the historical section as to its length, contents, and whether or not it was germane to the survey, Dr Wallace asked for a show of hands. A few were in favour of reducing it considerably but the majority voted that the whole section should be deleted; they considered history had little relation to the technical aspects of conservation.

Then, as chairman, Dr Wallace took the floor and with diplomacy and tact, said he did not agree; on the contrary, he said, he considered the section on history the most interesting in the report. It would, he said, go far to making the report more acceptable to a wide circle of readers. He then ruled that the section should be left in and any abridgement be left to Dr Marsh and me. With this excellent support from an eminent educator, it was evident that here was an open sesame to promote and encourage historical projects in the programmes of the authorities, if they should be formed.

The first interest in historical projects by the authorities was the placing of markers on sites of special significance. The Don Valley Conservation Authority gave leadership in this, due largely to the enthusiasm and energy of Mrs George Klinck, chairwoman of the historical sites advisory board. For most of these markers she was responsible for the historical research, preparing the presentation address and, in most cases, delivering it herself. When the four authorities in the Toronto region were merged into one and Mrs Dorothy Hague became chairwoman of the Metropolitan Toronto and Region Conservation Authority's historical sites advisory board, an historical markers sub-committee was appointed with Mrs Klinck in the chair.

The unveiling ceremonies at which the markers were presented were carried out with dignity. In most cases printed invitations were sent to those interested; the chairman of the authority or the historical sites advisory board usually presided, a local clergyman offered a prayer of dedication, and an address was delivered outlining the significance of the marker. The marker was then presented to the mayor or reeve of the municipality in which it was situated for safekeeping and maintenance.

When the authorities started to erect these markers, the government of Ontario gave a grant of fifty percent of the cost. In 1958, after the Ontario archeological and historical sites board was appointed and started its work of marking historical sites, the government stopped making grants to the authorities. However, Queen's Park said that authorities wishing to continue this programme should select sites and if these were approved by the sites board, it would erect one of its own standard markers. This ruling dampened the enthusiasm of the authorities, with the result that few markers have since been recommended. The ones which were erected by the authorities in the early days are: Ausable River Conservation Authority – Brewster's mill, Rock Glen, and St Anne's Church; Holland Valley Conservation

Twenty-six years after the pace-setting Guelph Conference, this group dedicated a plaque to the inspiration it provided. On 27 September 1967 the officials assembled at the Ganaraska's Garden Hill conservation area were C.R. Purcell; Professor A.F. Coventry; Dr A.H. Richardson; Mrs J.D. Thomas, widow of the Guelph Conference chairman; Professor A.W. Baker; and C.A. Walkinshaw.

Authority – the big anchor; the Metropolitan Toronto and Region Conservation Authority – Ashbridge family, Bloor's brewery, carriage road to Castle Frank, Castle Frank, Farr's mills, Haggart Brothers Agricultural Works, mill sites in the Don valley, Patterson village, Summerville settlement and the Thomson settlement; North Grey Conservation Authority – Inglis Falls grist and sawmill; and the Saugeen Valley Conservation Authority – Indian battleground.

GANARASKA REGION CONSERVATION AUTHORITY

Guelph Conference memorial

On 27 September 1967 the conservation authorities of Ontario dedicated a memorial to mark more than one-quarter of a century of conservation achievement in Ontario, begun by the Guelph Conference in 1941. The Guelph meeting gave birth to an outstanding project, the Ganaraska watershed survey, jointly sponsored by the government of Ontario and the government of Canada.

The memorial is situated in the Garden Hill conservation area and consists of an oval boulder approximately five-by-six feet, moved from the farm of O. Hilton

The Morrison Dam built by the Ausable authority.

Harris, chairman of the authority. This supports a bronze plaque bearing the names of the nine organizations which formed the conference.

In an interesting and moving ceremony conducted by James A. Reynolds, secretary-treasurer of the authority, Mrs J.D. Thomas, widow of the first chairman of the conference, unveiled the plaque. Dr A.H. Richardson gave the historical address and four other members of the conference – Professor A.W. Baker, Professor A.F. Coventry, C.A. Walkinshaw and C.R. Purcell – also spoke briefly. J. Grant Smith, chairman of the conservation authorities chairmen's committee, placed a time capsule containing pertinent documents beneath the stone as a permanent record.

Over the years several conservation authorities have created conservation areas and other facilities and named them for former members of the authority whose contributions have been outstanding. Although these memorials are not, in the strictest sense, historical, this seemed to be the best place to record them.

AUSABLE RIVER CONSERVATION AUTHORITY

Morrison Dam
This dam is situated on the main Ausable River above the town of Exeter and forms a small lake of 28 acres with sufficient fringe lands to create an attractive conservation area. Besides providing a small amount of flood control the dam provides fishing, swimming, boating and areas for family picnics.

It was officially opened on 4 June 1958 by the Honourable W.M. Nickle, QC, minister of planning and development. At a subsequent meeting of the members of the Ausable River Conservation Authority and many of his friends, tribute was paid Mr Morrison by presenting him with an oil painting of the dam and an illuminated scroll that reads: 'On this occasion, we the members of the Ausable River Conservation Authority hereby place on record our debt of gratitude and appreciation to

Four authorities have built or restored pioneer villages as part of a continuing public relations plan to acquaint the public with the aims of conservation. This example is part of the Fanshawe village near London.

John Alexander Morrison a member of the authority since its inception and chairman from 1951 to 1958, in recognition of his outstanding example of leadership and service in promoting the conservation of natural resources of Western Ontario.'

UPPER THAMES RIVER CONSERVATION AUTHORITY

Watson H. Porter pavilion
Known throughout Ontario, especially by the farming folk, as the editor of the *Farmer's Advocate*, Watson Porter was untiring in promoting the cause of conservation, not only through the medium of the editorial page but in numerous other effective methods as well. His superb organizational ability in promoting the Ontario Conservation and Reforestation Association has already been mentioned and when it became known that the municipalities on the Thames could become partners with the government in carrying out a broad programme of conservation in the Thames valley, Porter was appointed chairman of the steering committee which led to the forming of the Upper Thames River Conservation Authority; he was appointed the first secretary-treasurer.

The pavilion which is named in his honour is situated in the J. Cameron Wilson park on the fringe lands of the Fanshawe reservoir. Rustic in design with massive timbers, it fits in admirably with the surrounding parkland. On the large stone fireplace which is a focal point in the building, a plaque has been placed with the following inscription: 'This pavilion is named in honour of Watson H. Porter, first

secretary-treasurer of the Upper Thames River Conservation Authority in appreciation of his leadership in conservation.'

J. Cameron Wilson park

Dr J. Cameron Wilson, a physician and surgeon and a distinguished citizen of
London – he had been mayor in 1921 and member of the Ontario legislature for
South London during the period 1923–34 – was the first chairman of the Upper
Thames River Conservation Authority. He was a great leader and will always be
associated with the development of the authority in its early years. He succeeded in
drawing together all the municipalities concerned, an achievement that only his
political experience and diplomatic tact made possible.

Shortly after his election as chairman, he retired from his medical practice and
spent many hours of each day on authority business, which, at that time, was the
building of the Fanshawe Dam and the park. During their construction there was
hardly a day, when the weather was fine, that he was not out watching the progress,
and no doubt visualizing the well-being which they would contribute to the people
of the Thames valley in the years to come. Within the park the authority has
constructed the upper Thames pioneer village, one of three maintained by Ontario
authorities.

Dr Wilson's sincerity of purpose and appreciation of the problems at hand are
reflected in his annual chairman's reports and gave much encouragement to his
associates in the formative years of the authority. They always contained a pro-
nouncement inspirational in its content which is exemplified in his last report before
retirement: 'Never in my past experience have I seen the representatives of thirty-
one municipalities, of mixed rural and urban character, joined together in harmonious association and dedicated to the common purpose of conserving the natural
resources and improving the way of life of the people of a river valley. This
harmonious association has been the secret of our success and must be maintained
at all costs if we are to go forward and complete the vast programme you have laid
down for the next few years.'

Gordon W. Pittock Dam

Acknowledged as one of the leaders in conservation in Ontario, Gordon Pittock was
appointed representative from Ingersoll when the upper Thames authority was
formed. In 1950 he was appointed second vice-chairman to assist Dr Wilson; the
following year he became vice-chairman and in 1955 succeeded Dr Wilson as
chairman, which position he held until his resignation in 1965.

In the early years during the building of the Ingersoll channel, the first major
project of the authority, he did yeoman service in arranging the finances between the
authority and the industries upstream from Ingersoll which had been flooded during
the great flood of 1937, and for whom the channel was primarily built. He also
worked assiduously to bring about water control on the whole upper Thames
watershed which culminated in 1961 in the ten-year flood control agreements
between the governments of Canada and Ontario and the authority.

His interests went far beyond the boundaries of his own watershed. As a member of the Ontario legislature for four years, he served on the select committee on conservation authorities appointed by the legislature in 1965 and for a number of years was chairman of the Conservation Authorities Chairmen's Committee.

For these and many more contributions to the success of the authority, the flood-control dam at Woodstock was named in his honour.

R. Thomas Orr Dam

A prominent business man in the city of Stratford, Tom Orr was especially interested in the conservation of water and was one of the enthusiastic promoters of the Upper Thames River Conservation Authority. At the inaugural meeting he was elected vice-chairman and on his retirement was appointed honorary vice-chairman.

He is remembered mostly by the citizens of Stratford as one who helped give leadership in 1904 to the development of the city park system, which has as its central feature beautiful Lake Victoria, with a water surface of 44 acres and adjoining lands tastefully landscaped only a few hundred yards from the main street of the city – a unique and delightful development found all too rarely in urban planning.

The dam, which replaces an earlier one, holds back the waters of the Avon River (a tributary of the Thames) to form Lake Victoria. It was officially opened on 24 October 1967.

MOIRA RIVER CONSERVATION AUTHORITY

Colonel Roscoe Vanderwater conservation area

Situated two miles east of Thomasburg and seventeen miles north of Belleville, this area is a multi-purpose property, 631 acres in size with three miles of frontage on the lower reaches of the Moira River. Much of the area through which the river flows is wooded and in several places the flat limestone is near the surface which provides spectacular rapids during heavy flow.

The marker is a bronze tablet mounted on a cairn with the inscription: 'This conservation area was named in grateful appreciation of the contribution to conservation in Eastern Ontario by Colonel Roscoe Vanderwater, DSO, VD. It was through his interest and initiative that the Moira River Conservation Authority was formed and prospered. He served as its first chairman and was secretary-treasurer from 1948 to 1957.'

In the presence of Mrs Vanderwater, the area was officially opened on 1 August 1960 by the Honourable W.M. Nickle, QC, minister of the Department of Commerce and Development.

O'Hara's sawmill

Located near the town of Madoc, this old sawmill has been restored to operating order by the Moira river authority.

METROPOLITAN TORONTO AND REGION CONSERVATION AUTHORITY

Elmer Little tract in the Humber forest

Elmer Little was a farmer well known in Albion Township who for many years was active in the township council; besides being clerk for many years he also held other responsible positions. Early in the work of the Humber authority he was the pioneer in reforestation and personally negotiated the initial tracts of the Humber forest, now included in the Metropolitan Toronto and Region Conservation Authority forest of 1,673 acres. He was also responsible for initiating and extending the cooperative tree planting programme between private landowners and the authority.

Black Creek pioneer village

Located at the intersection of Jane Street and Steeles Avenue, this reconstructed pioneer village is a favourite with Toronto-area school children.

Roblin's mill

This grist and flour mill in operating condition is located within the Black Creek pioneer village (see above).

Catherine Scholes memorial library

Catherine Scholes was a leader in outdoor education in Ontario. Through her efforts the first outdoor classroom was established by the York Memorial Collegiate Institute. The movement culminated in the Albion Hills conservation school.

In the lounge of the Albion Hills conservation field centre hangs a portfolio of stone prints and a citation which reads: 'To the memory of Catherine Scholes (d December 4, 1960) distinguished teacher of girl's physical education, York Memorial Collegiate Institute, ornamental swimmer, canoeist, camper. Daughter of John L. Scholes and granddaughter of John Scholes in whose family are seven amateur world sports' records. She was at home with the waters and the woods and with the small things that grow and live there, and she knew their ways. She loved children and they loved her because they felt comfortable in her presence. This Albion Hills conservation school owes its existence to her inspiration. This portfolio of stone prints of some of her favourites of the waters and the woods was designed, executed and presented to the Catherine Scholes nature library by Alexander Millar, OACA, OSA, CGP, ex-student of York Memorial Collegiate Institute and a personal friend.'

Blanche Snell conservation library

Blanche Snell was also a leader with Catherine Scholes in outdoor education and was associated with her in the first outdoor educational experience held by the York Memorial Collegiate Institute, where both were highly respected teachers. The library which carries her name is in the Claremont conservation field centre.

GANARASKA REGION CONSERVATION AUTHORITY

Richardson lookout
In Dean's Hill conservation area, which is an oval, smoothly rounded hill (drumlin) with an elevation of approximately 850 feet above Lake Ontario, one may obtain a spectacular view of the Ganaraska watershed, Rice Lake and Lake Ontario. At the highest point of the hill is an observation platform.

The area was officially opened on 8 July 1964 by the Honourable J.R. Simonett, minister of energy and resources management.

LAKEHEAD REGION CONSERVATION AUTHORITY

Wishart conservation area
Comprising 530 acres, this area is named to honour Mrs Eunice Wishart, a former mayor of Port Arthur, an ardent conservationist, and a member of the Neebing authority, the predecessor of the Lakehead Region Conservation Authority. The property is traversed by the Current River and is well wooded with poplar, birch and spruce. In addition to picnic areas, outdoor education and forest management, the authority maintains a snowmobiling trail for family use.

Williams forest
At the inaugural meeting of the Lakehead Region Conservation Authority in 1963 a tract of 806 acres, part of the authority's agreement forest, was named to honour Frank Williams. The resolution which was adopted unanimously at the meeting reads: 'That in recognition of untiring and fruitful services toward the inception of a conservation authority in this area of Ontario, as a result of repeated overtures by the city of Fort William to the provincial government for flood relief; we hereby suitably honour a former chairman of the Neebing Valley Conservation Authority, Frank Williams, who served in this capacity since its inception in 1954 until the end of 1961. Such recognition to take the form of naming the following authority holdings in Oliver Township as "Williams Forest."'

HOLLAND VALLEY CONSERVATION AUTHORITY

Wesley Brooks memorial conservation area
Situated in the heart of Newmarket, this area was developed by the authority after Hurricane Hazel had destroyed the small dam in the town and ravaged the park which was adjacent to it. The area is 31 acres, including Fairy Lake which occupies seventeen. It is a pleasant spot in the centre of an urban community and has many uses. Although the lake is not suited for swimming, the authority has sponsored a wildlife programme of feeding mallards, red heads, wood ducks and Canada geese which provides much interest for the town folk especially the children. The park is also the centre for many community affairs and in winter the pond serves as the town skating rink.

These brief sketches of some of the outstanding attractions of certain conservation areas must, by their very brevity, neglect others. Without thinking too hard one can remember with fondness the Doon pioneer village in Waterloo County, a project partially sponsored by the Grand River Conservation Authority; Ball's grist and flour mill near Vineland, sponsored by the Niagara Peninsula Conservation Authority; and the John Backhouse grist and flour mill near Port Rowan, a project of the Big Creek Conservation Authority.

9

Proclaiming the Creed of Conservation

When the Conservation Branch was established there were a few municipalities which, because of the urgency of flood control in their areas, soon formed authorities and proceeded with their problems. But the programme envisioned went far beyond flood control. Therefore, one of the most important tasks of the branch in the early years was to proclaim this new philosophy of conservation, and to demonstrate how the programme could apply to all needy parts of Ontario.

Many of the minor methods used in any good public relations programme were employed. On the other hand, in some instances there were major efforts, a few of which will be looked at in detail.

As has been stated the conference on river valley development held in London, 13–14 October 1944, was such a success it was decided to hold two additional conferences, similar in educational content, in other parts of the province.

The first, for residents of Eastern Ontario, was held at Queen's University, Kingston in February 1945. The conference commenced on Friday, 2 February at 2:30 PM, the delegates being welcomed by the Honourable Dana Porter, minister of the Department of Planning and Development, Dr R.C. Wallace, principal of Queen's University, and His Worship C.L. Boyd, mayor of Kingston. Dr G.B. Langford, director of the Department of Planning and Development, was chairman for the first session at which the following papers were presented: 'Conservation in Southern Ontario,' by Professor R.F. Legett; 'Utilization of the Fish and Game Resources of Ontario,' by Professor W.J.K. Harkness; and 'The Need for Urban and Rural Cooperation in Conservation,' by Watson H. Porter.

At 7 PM, the delegates were tendered a complimentary banquet by the Department of Planning and Development in the university gymnasium at which Dr E.H. Graham, chief of the biological division, US Soil Conservation Service, Washington, DC, was guest speaker. Dr Graham's address was illustrated with slides followed by motion pictures showing water power, wildlife, modern methods of farm tillage, and kindred subjects.

At the Saturday morning session, H.S. Arkell, Britannia Heights, was chairman, and the following papers were presented: 'Forest Regions of Southern Ontario,' by G.M. Dallyn; 'Domestic Water Supply: Urban and Rural Problems,' by Dr John Wyllie; and 'Natural Regions in Eastern Ontario,' by Dr D.F. Putnam.

At noon on Saturday a complimentary luncheon was tendered by Queen's University in the University gymnasium, and the programme was in charge of the Ontario Conservation and Reforestation Association. The president, Dr J.H. Munro, Maxville, was in the chair. The speaker at Luncheon was Dr R.C. Wallace, principal of Queen's, following which Harry Sirrett, Brighton, chairman of Zone 4 of the Ontario Conservation and Reforestation Association presented Dr Wallace with a leather-bound volume of the Ganaraska report.

M.C. McPhail, principal of the Kemptville Agricultural School was chairman of the Saturday afternoon session at which the following papers were presented: 'The South Nation River and Its Environs,' by Ferdinand Larose; and 'Soil Conservation Practices,' by L.R. Webber.

The second conference to grow out of the original London meeting was requested by the community council's coordinating committee of the Toronto district to discuss problems of conservation in the Humber and Don watersheds, and was held in Toronto on 29–30 November 1946.

The conference commenced on a Friday at 2 PM, and the delegates were welcomed by A.H. Richardson, for the Honourable Dana Porter, minister of the Department of Planning and Development, who was in Mexico at the time. Professor R.F. Leggett was chairman of the first session, at which the following papers were presented: 'Forests of the Humber,' by A.S.L. Barnes; 'The Don Valley System,' by Dr D.F. Putnam and L.G. Reeds; and 'Soil Conservation Farming,' by Professor G.N. Ruhnke.

That evening a banquet was held in the Arcadian Court at which the guest speaker was the Honourable George A. Drew, QC, premier of Ontario. The premier's address was followed by a tableau entitled 'The Humber,' presented by the 77th Toronto Troop of Boy Scouts, and the evening concluded with two excellent conservation films.

At the Saturday morning session, W. Austin Peters, president of the Ontario Federation of Anglers and Hunters, was chairman, and the following papers were presented: 'A Land-Use Survey on the Etobicoke Creek,' by W.J.P. Creswick; 'Fish Studies in Southern Ontario,' by Dr A.G. Huntsman; and 'Conservation on the Farm Property,' by M.A. Adamson.

At noon the second day a conference luncheon was held with N.A. Fletcher, then president of the Ontario Conservation and Reforestation Association, in the chair. Following the luncheon Mr Fletcher briefly outlined the achievements of the OCRA since its inception in 1937 and Watson H. Porter, secretary of the OCRA presented a paper entitled 'Europe is Telling Us.'

Eric W. Baker was chairman for the Saturday afternoon session at which the following papers were presented: 'Regional Planning,' by F.G. Gardiner, KC, 'Recreation on Forest Lands,' by Professor J.L. Van Camp; and 'Recreation on the Humber,' by K.M. Mayall.

An interesting feature of both conferences was an exhibition of approximately one hundred photographic enlargements, maps, bulletins and books, loaned by government departments and delegates. These were studied carefully by the delegates and helped to supplement the information which was presented by the various speakers.

The papers read at these two conferences were published in bulletins with many pictures and attractive covers, and were distributed widely over the province. Together with help of the press, they brought the subject of conservation favourably before the public.

THE MUSKINGUM TOUR

A conference provides a good introduction to basic problems but, at its best, it is a static function. What was needed for the members of the authorities was an on-site demonstration of projects which had already been accomplished by an organization which had problems analogous to Ontario. Accordingly, in 1948 a programme of tours was inaugurated which had this purpose in mind, the first being to the Muskingum Conservancy District in Ohio.

As this first tour was a milestone in conservation education and opened new vistas of what could be done in Ontario in the years to come, it is appropriate that it be described fully (with minor editing) by one who had a deep and abiding interest in this important work – Watson Porter.

On Monday, 27 September 1948, two buses started rolling toward Ohio and in the large highway vehicles were representatives of the conservation authorities now established in eleven river valleys in Ontario. The destination was New Philadelphia, Ohio, where they were welcomed by Bryce Browning, chief administrative officer of the Muskingum Conservancy District, who with his staff, showed the pilgrims over the huge Muskingum watershed and explained the many flood-control and conservation projects which are combined in a functioning scheme unsurpassed in North America.

There, on a watershed spread across more than 8,000 square miles, the Ontario delegates saw dams (earth-filled and concrete), man-made lakes, farm ponds, reforestation, strip-cropping and contour cultivation, grassed waterways, large research enterprises to measure the runoff of soil and water, and recreational facilities that are now producing a handsome revenue for the Muskingum Conservancy District. The delegates saw not a finished product – no conservation project is ever finished – but they did have an opportunity to study a vast enterprise begun fifteen years ago and that for at least ten years has been a functioning scheme. Almost everywhere they saw evidences of conservation farming, and they saw source waters so successfully controlled that urban centres and countryside are now protected from flood losses. Frank Crume, the capable and genial district officer who acted as guide, expressed it this way: 'Nowadays people don't know there's a flood on unless they read it in the newspapers, whereas in the old days they'd be fleeing to the hills.'

The tour was sponsored, organized and partly financed by the Ontario Department of Planning and Development. The government provided the transportation and all the arrangements were made by the staff.

When the buses rolled into Ashland, Ohio, the delegates were met by C.D. Blubaugh, a farmer who restored an abandoned property and made it the most famous farm in North America. From then on, the first call was at Malabar Farm about which millions of people have read in *Pleasant Valley* and *Malabar Farm*, by Louis Bromfield.

Of the fourteen dams operated by the conservancy, only a few were inspected. These are located strategically, mostly on small streams with a view to the control of source waters which has been so successfully achieved that flood damage is no longer feared. In fact, the district enjoys a wide margin of safety in the storage space provided behind the dams. This phase of the Muskingum programme was a revelation, not so much from an engineering point of view, but rather because the system of storage basins produces by-products of great value. In most cases lakes are created and held on the higher elevations in the vast valley of the Muskingum and its tributaries and deep seepage from the impounded water helps to maintain an underground supply which is invaluable.

Still another by-product is recreation. Ohio is not blessed with inland waters and the people of the state are flocking to these man-made lakes to fish and hunt, swim and play. The district is now organizing this recreation and charging what Bryce Browning calls a 'service fee.' Already, recreation is bringing in a handsome revenue and it is expected that the annual returns from the lakes in the years ahead will go a long way in meeting the maintenance costs of the entire enterprise.

The district owns 65,000 acres of land of which 22,000 acres have agricultural possibilities and are rented to farmers. But it is not the policy of the district to engage in the farming business. 'Farmers can do a better job at that,' the officials say.

With regard to forestry, a different view is held. Non-agricultural land is being rapidly planted and the aim is to maintain a good percentage of forest cover in the neighbourhood of all the lakes. The district has considerable areas of commercial timber and sales of these bring in a nice income, but nothing less than eighteen inches in diameter is cut. Oil and coal leases also account for a sizeable revenue.

Runoff creates floods and the Muskingum engineers are facing up to the problem right at its source. Not only are they encouraging strip-cropping, contour cultivation and permanent grass to make the water walk rather than run downhill, but they are planting gorests on the hilltops and hillsides to create an absorptive forest floor that will suck in the water and deliver it to lower soil strata rather than directly into the streams. Responsibility for this part of the programme devolves upon H.P. Garritt who tramped the delegates over farms and hillsides on the last forenoon of their visit in Ohio to show them first, a plough designed to turn up a high ridge which will hold two inches of run-off on which the trees are planted; and then a tree-planting machine with the aid of which a crew will plant 10,000 trees in eight hours. Both implements work on quite steep slopes – anything up to 45 percent grade, Garritt told us.

An interesting feature of this demonstration was the Muskingum practice of planting on *top* of the upturned furrow rather than *in* the furrow, as has been the custom here and elsewhere. The ridge is made in the year previous to the planting.

The Muskingum plan involves more than dams. Throughout the whole tour of the watershed, attention was constantly directed to soil-building processes, to the checking of runoff waters and to the control of soil erosion. Most revealing was a visit to the 1,000-acre hydrologic research station at Fresno which is conducted by the United States Soil Conservation Service.

After the first Muskingum tour, other tours were held almost every second year.

In the early years when on tour, one evening was given over for a conference. However, by 1956 there were so many important matters to discuss that a conference lasting two to three days in alternating years was inaugurated. Since then the conference has become an important function of the authorities, a forum at which matters affecting the authorities can be discussed and decisions made. Besides being a workshop for the authorities, papers are given on pertinent subjects, outside speakers are invited to address the conference and a highlight of the occasion is a one-day bus trip visiting important projects of the host authority.

CONSERVATION AUTHORITIES TOURS, BIENNIAL CONFERENCES

Year	Function	Location	Host
1948	1st Tour & Conference	Muskingum, Ohio	Conservation branch
1950	2nd Tour & Conference	New York state	Conservation branch
1952	3rd Tour & Conference	Southern Ontario	Conservation branch
1954	4th Tour & Conference	Muskingum, Ohio	Conservation branch
1956	5th Conference	London	Upper Thames River
1957	5th Tour	St Lawrence Seaway	Metropolitan Toronto & Region Conservation Authority
1958	6th Conference	Toronto	Conservation branch
1960	7th Conference	Preston	Grand valley
1962	8th Conference	Toronto	Metropolitan Toronto & Region Conservation Authority
1963	6th Tour	Muskingum, Ohio	
1964	9th Conference	Vineland	Niagara region
1965	7th Tour	Tennessee Valley Authority	
1966	10th Conference	Hamilton	Halton region
1967	8th Tour	Western Canada	
1968	11th Conference	Peterborough	Otonabee region
1969	9th Tour	Maritime provinces	
1970	12th Conference	Sudbury	Junction Creek

THE CONSERVATION SURVEY

The conservation survey which was carried out by the Conservation Branch was also a useful form of public relations, not only because it produced a report which was a working plan for the years ahead, but while it was in progress it was a forthright and obvious sign that flood problems were being studied in the watershed. The technical staff dealing with hydraulics, forestry, land use, wildlife and recreation transferred from head office to the camp which, in the early days, was under canvas, and with the assistance of about forty students from the universities carried out the field work.

When any particular survey was well under way, a press day was held for the local papers during which the techniques were demonstrated and areas where conservation could be practised were visited. In addition, another day was spent

G.W. Pittock, chairman of the UTRCA, Watson H. Porter, editor of the *Farmer's Advocate*, L.N. Johnson, secretary treasurer of the UTRCA, Bruce Browning, secretary treasurer of the Muskingum Conservancy district, Ohio, and Dr G.B. Langford, formerly director of the Ontario Department of Planning and Development, review a landmark publication, the Upper Thames Valley Conservation Report of 1952.

touring the watershed with members of the authority and the members of the municipal councils which were included in the authority. The day of the tour commenced with lunch in camp, followed by brief addresses describing the methods of the survey, after which the whole group in cars toured the watershed and were shown troublesome areas where conservation practices could be carried out.

Furthermore, the presentation of the conservation report was a special occasion. It began with a dinner for the authority, then came a public meeting, to which 150 or more interested citizens were invited by printed invitation, and at which the minister presented the report, a copy of which was given to each member of the authority. Following the presentation the guests were invited to inspect a display of maps, charts and photographs which were explained by the technical staff.

Later, if funds were available, an attractive bulletin was published summarizing the report and about 3,000 were distributed in the watershed.

PERIODICALS

Early in the work of the authorities, it was decided to publish a newsletter which would serve at least three purposes: to inform all authorities regarding the projects being carried out province-wide; to be a useful piece of publicity for each authority; and to serve as a record of the progress of the authorities over the years.

The word 'newsletter' did not adequately suit the type of publication which was planned and it was necessary to search for a more original title. It so happened that at this time Lloyd Baxter, who was the branch photographer, had made a short film for the Humber Valley Conservation Authority with the title, *Our Valley*. This was considered an appropriate title for the new publication, and it was so named.

The first copies of *Our Valley* were mimeographed on legal-size paper and were issued at the request of each authority. The first number was for the upper Thames in March 1952 and from then until June 1954 thirteen authorities were served in this way. By this time the demand for extra copies became so great that there was very little difference in cost between mimeographing and printing. The Honourable W.K. Warrender, minister at that time, authorized the printing of the publication with the result that the first edition in this new form was issued in January 1955.

Our Valley was designed, written and edited by the conservation staff. The field officers fed material to Herb Crown, the artwork was done by the chief draughtsman, the photographs were taken, for the most part, by the branch photographer, and the proofs were read by the stenographers. The front cover, and occasionally the endpapers, carried a suitable four-colour reproduction of a painting by a well-known Canadian artist loaned by the Rous and Mann Press, the printers, and an extra colour was used sparingly throughout the book. It was government bulletin size, published twice yearly in summer and winter, ran to between sixty and eighty pages and had lots of pictures. It was distributed free to all council members of municipalities which were included in the authorities, to government departments, interested organizations and individuals. Extra copies for distribution by the authorities were supplied at cost.

A practice which *Our Valley* introduced was a pithy, thought-provoking quotation displayed on the back cover. And to make it more intriguing, the author was a fictitious character named Samuel Woodstock. These 'quotations' were used widely; five are quoted below:

River valley development is the wise use of all the natural resources of a river valley for all the people living in the valley, for all time.

My son, I admonish you to cherish the little waters, for these replenish the mighty rivers that nourish our thirsty land.

I am convinced that these swamps, bogs and marshes were ordained from the beginning in the divine order of things to be left as natural reservoirs, and much heart-searching and thought should be exercised before they are discarded for some other use.

As I contemplate the teeming thousands who will come to our fair province in the years that lie ahead, and realize the paucity of open spaces for their healthful recreation, I fear that we who call ourselves conservationists today will be grouped with those who condemned the great Socrates, whose names are now forgotten but are remembered only for their dullness of apprehension.

It is well for man to rest from his labours and partake of the fruits of this bountiful land, let us give thanks, for they are the gift of God, Amen.

The first of these sayings of Samuel Woodstock's was composed for the convention held in London 13–14 October 1944. The second was written with the small

Ganaraska River, and its many tributaries, in mind. The third appeared at the time of the annual meeting of the Federation of Ontario Naturalists held in Toronto in 1952, the theme of which was the preservation of wetlands. The fourth was written at the time several groups were pressing for much more expansion in recreation in Ontario. The fifth was a 'grace before meat' to be used at authorities' dinners.

In 1966 the Conservation Authorities Branch published a new magazine titled, *Watersheds*. The purpose of this new venture is best told by quoting a message from the Honourable J.R. Simonett, minister of the Department of Energy and Resources Management at that time.

'I am very pleased to present to you the first edition of our new publication *Watersheds*. This project has been undertaken in response to numerous requests from conservation authorities and is designed to provide up-to-date information on all facets of conservation work in Ontario.

I trust that you will find this and future issues of *Watersheds* both interesting and informative. Its success depends on all authority members, and I call on you to support the undertaking by submitting articles and ideas for publication. It is our hope that *Watersheds* will help maintain interest in conservation at a high level and that your individual authority administrations will benefit from the information it contains.

Also, to quote A.S.L. Barnes, director of the Conservation Authorities Branch, in the first number of *Watersheds*:

'The whole gathering ground of a river system,' is one of the dictionary meanings of the word 'watershed.' How appropriately it defines the area over which a conservation authority carries out its work. Ideally it conjures up a picture of wooded hillsides sheltering tiny springs; of swamps holding water which is released gradually to the river system; of well-managed farmlands where water runs slowly down slopes and grassed waterways; of river channels free of eroding banks, and finally the river itself emptying into a great inland lake. In addition are the man-made works erected to regulate the waters which nature provides in such abundance in Ontario.

Watersheds is the successor to *Our Valley*, though it makes no attempt to duplicate that combination of qualities which made the former publication a source of pleasure and admiration to all who read it. However, there are those who will recall that *Our Valley* itself began as a legal-size mimeographed leaflet which changed in 1953 under the able editorship of Dr A.H. Richardson, to the handsome brochure which was published semi-annually until 1961.

Watersheds is an attractive magazine, letter size with many illustrations; the editor is fortunate in being able to use plenty of colour. The magazine amply fulfills the purpose set forth by the minister of the department and by the director of the Conservation Authorities Branch.

10

Capturing Youth's Imagination

For more years than many of us can remember, the naturalists of Ontario – both professional and amateur – have tried to instil in the youth of this province a heightened regard for the complex interrelationship of man, animals and landscape that we call nature. That their efforts have been successful is self-evident; today's youth can and do speak with knowledge and discernment about 'ecology,' 'environmental factors' and 'recycling of waste.' Anyone who has been even slightly involved with a natural history society or bird-watchers' club can testify to the active participation of the young.

As much as anyone, the late Stuart L. Thompson was responsible for bringing young people into the conservation movement. Thompson lived in Toronto but was known in many parts of Ontario for his talks on nature subjects. He was a skilled amateur naturalist who, besides being a keen observer, had the remarkable ability to imitate accurately the calls and songs of our native birds. One of his pleasures was to take groups of boys on nature hikes up the Don valley, the locale of some of the animal stories written by his famous uncle, Ernest Thompson-Seton. During the many years in which he conducted these trips, hundreds of boys learned their first lessons in conservation.

In the summer 1958 edition of *Our Valley* is a picture taken by Stuart Thompson in 1910, showing a group of his young friends on one of these nature rambles. Included in the picture is a nine-year-old lad who later became a distinguished member of the Ontario cabinet and, later, the chief justice of Ontario. One of his achievements as a minister was that he laid the foundation of the conservation movement in Ontario. He was the late Honourable Dana Porter, QC, first minister of the Department of Planning and Development.

Some of the methods used to interest school children in nature study are nature trails, nature hikes, arbor days, reforestation planting, visits to woodlots, visits to sugarbush operations, fishing days, bus trips to acquaint the children with the activities of their own authority, the making of wood-duck boxes and bluebird houses, scrapbook competitions – usually a class effort – public speaking and essay

The Don valley authority established a fifty-mile trail in the 1950s that was toured by thousands of school children from the Toronto area.

contests. To assist in the public speaking and essay contests, one small authority placed 140 books on conservation in the school libraries of its watersheds.

In 1959 the Kiwanis Club of Owen Sound and North Grey Region Conservation Authority conducted an essay contest in the public schools of the Owen Sound district in which fifty-seven pupils participated.

The most elaborate conservation trail laid out by an authority was the Don valley conservation trail of the early 1950s. It commenced at the mouth of the Don River and meandered approximately fifty miles up the east side of the watershed to a point six miles north of Richmond Hill. It had twenty-four stations marked by attractive signs supported on posts ten feet high, each sign portraying one or more phases of conservation. For guidance the authority published a fifty-six-page booklet in which was a picture of each station and on the opposite page a description of what to look for. The booklet was not only a guide to the trail but was also used afterwards as a conservation primer. For the most part the trail was used by groups of Grade 7 and 8 school children from Toronto schools. In the first two years the trail was open 7,000 pupils in 200 bus loads travelled over it.

Today, when problems of pollution are being given priority by the three senior governments, it is of interest to describe Station No. 1 on this trail. The illustration is a picture of the filthy mouth of the Don River; the description, written twenty years ago, is:

The lower part of the Don River has been straightened and its banks have been protected by man-made walls, so that its present mouth provides accommodation for a great number of ships which bring cargoes of coal, oil and other products to Toronto.

The river is badly polluted by sewage and industrial wastes, and by large quantities of floating rubbish. In mid-summer, the flow of water is not sufficient to clean out the channel;

The mouth of the Don River in 1952. The authority's pamphlet put the problem baldly: '... There is often ... more sewage than river water in this part of the Don.' In the late eighteenth century Mrs John Graves Simcoe saw salmon being taken from this stretch of the Don.

consequently, there is often, at this time of the year, more sewage than river water in this part of the Don. It is one of the most heavily polluted rivers in Ontario. At times, when the level of Lake Ontario is high, there is almost no current through the channel and the effects of the pollution become even worse. Such a river is a menace to health and is unfit for swimming and fishing. It is unattractive to the eye and has a bad odour.

The most necessary measure of conservation for the Don is to stop pollution at every point where it now enters the river. In addition, reforestation of the headwaters area would assist in regulating the flow of water and thereby keep the river clean.

When the Don trail was planned it was intended that the students would take one whole day on the trip. It was also hoped that a few acres with some conservation potential could be purchased and serve as a half-way house where the participants could take a break from bus travelling, have lunch, and view some conservation projects. But twenty years ago, it was difficult to engender enthusiasm for conservation. The school authorities limited the bus trip to one-half day, which constricted the programme; the authority lost interest and the trail was abandoned.

A popular and continuous form of education among the older youth has been the annual land judging contests. The rules of the contest read, 'Land judging helps develop an understanding of soil conservation; it helps point the way to intelligent

In 1955 the conservation authorities inaugurated soil-judging competitions for high school students. The competitions stimulated the boys and helped drive home the tenets of conservation.

management of land. The goal of land judging is to teach the participants to recognize the factors inherent in soils that determine their capabilities and how these factors, such as drainage and texture, affect soil management and cropping practices.' The contests are organized on a county basis in order to bring the agricultural representative of the Department of Agriculture and Food into the ambit of planning.

The first such contest was held in Peel County in 1955 and was planned jointly by Ken Higgs, who at the time was the field officer of the Humber authority, and James McCullough, who was the agricultural representative in Peel. In 1965, the tenth anniversary of the programme, the friends of Ken Higgs in the former Humber authority established a challenge trophy in his honour. It takes the form of a shield on which the names of the winners of the competition are engraved.

Many boys participate in organizations which have conservation as part of their on-going activities. There is little opportunity for most of them to participate in conservation projects at a more advanced level. The junior conservationist award programme is an attempt to fill this need.

The junior conservationist programme is sponsored by the Ontario Department of Energy and Resources Management. Its expressed objective is 'to provide an opportunity for boys to increase their knowledge and appreciation for their natural environment and its management.' Participation is limited to twenty-four boys each

Ken Higgs (right) accepts from Grant Henderson the Higgs shield, annually awarded in his honour to the winning student in soil-judging competitions.

summer – admittedly a very small number. But expectations are that the experience provided will help to develop future citizen leaders in the campaign for a better environment. A number of young conservationists from each year's programme have selected some aspect of resources management as their choice of career. Several who have spent their summers working for the Conservation Authorities branch have later gone on to universities and become professional resources managers.

The programme was started as an experiment in 1966 with ten participants. The award aspect of the programme is emphasized: the participants are selected from boys nominated by sponsoring organizations, and any organization with a continuing programme in conservation is encouraged to make nominations. Cooperating organizations include the Ontario Forestry Association and their resource rangers, nature clubs affiliated with the Federation of Ontario Naturalists, fish and game clubs associated with the Federation of Anglers and Hunters, 4-H Clubs of the Department of Agriculture and Food, Boy Scouts, and clubs and groups within secondary schools. Conservation authorities have also sponsored participants.

The Junior Conservationist programme is organized as a work and learning experience. Instruction is combined with discussions and field trips to provide

One year's participants in the junior conservationist award programme at the camp
in the Albion Hills conservation area.

information on all aspects of renewable resources management. Experts in various
fields are brought in during the first two weeks. While the main purpose of the
programme is to improve the participants' knowledge and observation of conservation and resources management, the experience of living together is an important
by-product. Programme arrangements are such that some of the boys have to do
their own 'housekeeping' including cooking.

The first week of the programme takes place at the Albion Hills conservation
field centre of the Metropolitan Toronto and Region Conservation Authority. It is
followed by visits to the University of Guelph and to a community college, together
with tours to conservation authority projects on the Credit, Halton and Grand
Rivers.

In 1970, the boys gathered at the Albion Hills conservation field centre on the
evening of the last Sunday in June. Registration, getting acquainted at a wiener
roast, followed by a midnight hike through the Albion Hills conservation area,
launched them into the activity. During this week at the field centre they received
intensive instruction in conservation practices and problems – forestry, wildlife
management, land use, water control and geology. Trips to the McLaughlin
planetarium, the Pickering nuclear station, swimming, fishing and shooting at the
Cold Creek conservation area provided a change of pace.

In their second week, the University of Guelph was the activity centre. Instruction and discussions with staff of the departments of soil science, crop science, and wildlife management brought more new information and viewpoints. There were trips off-campus to study land use planning in the Beaver valley with Mac Kirk, resources manager of North Grey Region Conservation Authority, conservation and planning in Whiteman's Creek on the Grand with Dick Patrick of the Grand River Conservation Authority, and a look at the birds and mammals in Kortright wildlife park near Guelph.

A weekend camping trip to Killbear provincial park near Parry Sound preceded five weeks spent on projects. In each case the project was to study all aspects of resource use in a small watershed. Agricultural and urban development, water management, wetlands, and recreation were examined and recorded.

The boys were given a voice in planning the methods and procedures of these watershed studies. Aerial photographs and topographic maps, compasses and binoculars were their most useful tools. Each landowner living in the watersheds to be studied was contacted, either by a visit from a programme leader or by letter before the programme got under way. The boys were encouraged to talk to the landowners and discuss with them their conservation viewpoints and recommendations. With but few exceptions the landowners were cooperative and interested in the study.

Youth's concern with social problems is reflected in protest marches, campus unrest and in 'opting out.' Some young people, however, voice their protest in a positive way and become active with organizations involved in environmental protection. The junior conservationist award programme helps at least two dozen young men every year to translate their dissatisfaction into positive action.

One youth group which deserves honourable mention is the Boy Scouts Association of Ontario. Its interest in conservation goes back to the years when this subject was not as popular as it is today. As early as 1928 and continuing for ten years the reforestation division of the Department of Lands and Forests held annual forestry camps over the 24 May holiday at the tree seed extracting plant at Angus in Simcoe County. The number of Boy Scouts at these camps averaged 125 annually and although the activities included were much the same as those carried out in conservation schools today, most emphasis was placed on reforestation. During the years these camps were held, approximately 250,000 trees were planted on public land in Simcoe County. In one year when the holiday fell on a weekend and the camp operated for four days, the scouts planted 60,000 trees.

When the conservation authorities came into being, the scouts were quick to offer their assistance in tree planting. The first plantings on the Ganaraska forest were done by Boy Scouts during a weekend camp. In 1955, in return for their enthusiastic assistance and as a 'thank you' for work well done, the Humber, Grand, Upper Thames and Don authorities collaborated with the Conservation Branch in the preparation of a bulletin in order that young Scouts might more easily obtain their forester proficiency badge.

In 1956, conservation was a national theme for Boy Scouts across Canada, and the scouts of Ontario played an important part. Projects included tree planting, making nesting boxes and feeding stations for birds, clearing debris from river

Uniformed Boy Scouts take part in a tree-planting weekend in the Ganaraska forest. On one 24 May weekend the scouts planted 60,000 seedlings.

banks, clearing farmland of debris after Hurricane Hazel, building small dams and bridges and assisting in the reclamation of historical sites. In that year, also the scouts' national council added four new proficiency badges – soil, water, forest and wildlife. To assist the scouts in earning these, the Conservation Branch cooperated with fifteen authorities in the preparation of a sixty-eight-page bulletin written by A.S.L. Barnes covering these four subjects. This bulletin also contained the following message:

In this great province of Ontario we have a heritage of natural resources more magnificent than our most optimistic forefathers dreamed. Modern science has given us the tools with which it can be either destroyed or developed at a far greater rate than was ever possible in the past. Boy Scouts have always made worthwhile contributions toward the wise use of our renewable natural resources, and it is my earnest hope that this booklet will help you to continue this good work. There is no better way in which a Scout can do his duty to God and the Queen than by carrying out a conservation good turn.

TORONTO, 16 APRIL 1956

W.M. NICKLE, QC

MINISTER, DEPARTMENT OF PLANNING AND DEVELOPMENT

In 1953 when the Humber was a separate authority, two members of the staff of York Memorial Collegiate Institute put in train their ideas of outdoor education, which culminated in the establishing of the Albion Hills conservation school. Many now consider it the most important programme of the Metropolitan Toronto and Region Conservation Authority.

In that year, Catherine Scholes, who had been in the physical education department of York Memorial, had retired. During her teaching career Miss Scholes had assisted in outdoor education in girl camps, and she enlisted the cooperation of her colleague, Blanche Snell, to promote a similar venture in public schools. Before consolidating their ideas, these two dedicated teachers visited schools in Great Britain where similar methods were practised. Subsequently, Kenneth Higgs, field officer of the Humber authority, was brought into their counsel and the final arrangements were made. From then the camps were promoted as a programme of the authority.

The campers were girls and boys of Grade 9 at York Memorial, with students from Grades 13 and teachers serving as counsellors. The campers numbered thirty-five and the period of study was three days – Wednesday to Friday in the latter part of May. Before camp opened much classroom time was spent discussing the programme of study and the schedule to be followed so that camp routine would be as effortless as possible. The subjects covered forest mapping, tree identification, principles of reforestation and woodlot management, pond and stream life, and an introduction to problems of water. Land-use problems were stressed including land capabilities and soil profiles; visits were made to individual farms specializing in dairy cattle, beef cattle, sheep and hogs. On these trips around the countryside a limited amount of the history of the Humber watershed was discussed. Friday afternoon was spent visiting a rural school, ending with a discussion on rural versus city living.

Those who attended these camps in the early years recall some aspects of pioneer living. The cabins leaked; the campgrounds had few of the comfortable amenities found in camps today, and in one year there was three inches of snow on the ground. But in spite of the drawbacks, when spring blossomed, (such is the resilience of youth) there were plenty of applicants for the camp.

The parents of campers were greatly interested in this type of education and were helpful with transportation. The farmers whom the young people visited, were cooperative in displaying the fine points of their well-bred stock and in explaining the complexities of farm management.

During the years when these camps were held under somewhat primitive conditions, many young people not only learned some of the basic principles of conservation, but also how to cooperate effectively as a group. When the success of the programme became evident, those who had sponsored it began to dream that some day a suitable building would be erected to house the activities. After eleven years of temporary quarters, the dream took shape and with the assistance of the Metropolitan Toronto and Region Conservation Foundation, a permanent school building became a reality.

The site selected was a secluded spot among the gently rolling hills of Albion Township in the Humber valley, where, in 1956, the authority had acquired its first conservation property, now enlarged to 927 acres and named the Albion Hills conservation area. The building is modern in design, approximately 148-by-50 feet, one floor with a basement. The most important rooms are a large combination dining room-activity area, lounge, laboratory, library, kitchen and sleeping quarters for forty students and staff. The groundbreaking ceremonies took place 21

The Albion Hills conservation field centre, home of the Albion Hills conservation school.

November 1962, with the first sod turned by the Honourable William G. Davis, minister of education at the time. The subject of his address was 'Outdoor Education' and ended:

Conservation is more than a subject, be it taught in or out-of-doors. It has a spiritual and emotional connotation. It is an attitude of mind as it is involved in man's finer feelings and aesthetic appreciation. Nature's beauty does much to make man think, and living so close to nature as pupils will do in this school camp in years to come, let us hope that they will gain this love for nature's gifts and gain a sense of responsibility towards the intelligent use of our natural resources.

May this school, the result of much hard work by the Metropolitan Toronto and Region Conservation Authority, prosper. May its influence spread so that young pupils will enjoy a love for the out-of-doors, establish lasting friendships, gain new knowledge and learn through conservation to become responsible citizens and respect and love their country. It is because I feel so strongly about these matters that I am particularly pleased to have this opportunity to participate in the programme today and to turn the first sod for the building of this school camp in the Albion Hills.

When it became known that the Albion school would become a reality, Blanche Snell was requested to write a calendar, with the assistance of the authority staff, 'to establish a conceptual framework which will provide guidelines for the operation of the school, the curriculum under broad headings, and the necessary pre-planning of students that must be accomplished by the homeroom teacher before their week at the school.' This task was done carefully and well, and is contained in a forty-six page booklet published by the authority.

Following the success of the school on the western section of the watershed, the Metropolitan Toronto and Region Conservation Authority, in 1970, opened a similar unit in the eastern section. Located in the Claremont conservation area it is named the Claremont conservation field centre. To conform with the name of the

The Ausable authority has preserved the gorge at Rock Glen, one of the finest outcroppings of Devonian fossils in North America. Students of geology and paleontology flock to study this 'nature's textbook.'

new unit, and the Cold Creek conservation field centre (a day-use educational facility), the name of Albion Hills school was changed to Albion Hills conservation field centre.

After observing the success of the first facility of this kind, other authorities were quick to see the advantages of such a programme. The first of these was sponsored by the Ausable River Conservation Authority in 1963. Under the leadership of Terry McCauley, who was field officer at that time, and with the liberal assistance of the London district Boy Scouts who offered their 400-acre Camp Sylvan for the camp site, a two-and-one-half day programme was begun.

Since then, nine authorities have carried out programmes of this kind, the camp period varying in length from one day to a week or more. The Hamilton Region Conservation Authority acquired its own property on which it established a re-source management centre for outdoor education. In addition, three authorities have appointed educational coordinators to their staffs. Nearly 100,000 of Ontario's young people are exposed to one or another of these educational programmes *every year*; in many authorities, where flood control and conservation techniques have been thoroughly explored, these outdoor classrooms have become the *major* part of the authority's programme.

It is not unreasonable to hope that the coming generations of young people in this province will be better equipped to understand and cope with the complexities of conservation than the older generations have been.

11

... for the Next Twenty-five Years

The Conservation Authorities Act of 1946, sets forth what an authority may do and what it may not do within its watershed. When it was written, the authors included all the problems which were urgent at the time and anticipated others which they believed might arise in the future. Thus, as the program got under way, amendments were made to the act to meet changing conditions. Some of the changes are of minor importance and may be considered as a tidying-up process; others which have to do with the administration of the Conservation Authorities Branch have little or no bearing on the story and will also be omitted; those which have a direct bearing on the progress and achievements of the authorities will be discussed at some length.

1952

In this year a very important amendment was added to Section 1(a) of the act, 'administration costs.' This subsection has been described as ambiguous because of the phrase 'administration costs,' but it should be noted that the phrase was placed in quotations by the law-makers and its meaning was spelled out by naming a number of specific projects and ending with the omnibus clause, 'and all expenditures necessary for carrying out the conservation work of the authority other than capital expenses and maintenance of approved schemes.'

The events leading up to the passing of this amendment are perhaps the most interesting in the early years of the authorities. On 7 April 1949 the Ontario legislature appointed a select committee on conservation which reported the next year and published its illustrated report with eighty-four recommendations. The report covered the gamut of conservation and, besides fulfilling a need as a conservation reader, was a valuable source of procedure for authorities, enhanced by the fact that its recommendations carried quasi-governmental approval. The big problem for the authorities was to clear the hurdle of costs which the projects in the report recommended, as the only governmental grants at this time were for flood control and authority forests. Some additional financial assistance was needed to make it possible to carry out these smaller schemes.

At this time Watson Porter of London was urging Dr J. Cameron Wilson, chairman of the upper Thames River authority, to extend the work into more general phases of conservation, particularly projects related to farm use. In 1951 Dr G.H. Jose, who was chairman of the advisory board of finance of the upper Thames, came to Toronto to discuss this matter because it was the responsibility of his board to find ways for financing these projects. He pointed out that small projects, including land use, rebuilding old mill dams, small picnic areas, community and farm ponds, and aid to those wishing to reforest their own properties, was an excellent way to sustain the interest of member municipalities. It was suggested that as the grant for the purchase of land for authority forests was 50 percent, that the government might make the same grant for these smaller needy projects. The best way to achieve this end, Dr Jose decided, would be to decide on how much the authority could raise on its own, describe the projects in detail, prepare a brief and send a strong delegation to the government asking for consideration. The total amound decided on was $40,000 divided equally between the government and the upper Thames authority. The brief also requested that a technical member of the Conservation Branch be seconded to the upper Thames authority to act as a field officer and coordinate the conservation schemes of the authority.

The delegation met the Honourable William Griesinger, minister of planning and development, and the Honourable Fletcher Thomas, minister of public works, the latter having been the chairman of the select committee on conservation. The two ministers were favourable to the proposal and brought the Honourable W.S. Gemmell, minister of lands and forests, into their counsel with the result that the cabinet authorized the grant. It is interesting to recall that the government was prepared to contribute *more* than $20,000 but this matching amount was the limit that the authority could hope to raise.

The next year the upper Thames again asked for consideration and as the 'grapevine' between authorities was very efficient, two other authorities asked for the same consideration. The Honourable William Griesinger recalled that he had made such grants to the upper Thames the year before and remarked, 'I assume that this is what is called establishing a policy and I will recommend the same for the Thames this year and all other authorities which wish to apply.' This was the big break-through respecting grants for the multiplicity of small – and not so small – schemes which are being carried out so successfully today.

The request for a field officer was also granted, and Leonard Johnson was seconded to the authority with the arrangement that the Department of Planning and Development would pay his salary and the authority defray his travelling and office expenses. This was the beginning of the appointment of field officers (resources managers) to the authorities.

1954
The amendment regarding recreation – which has already been dealt with in the chapter on that subject – was passed.

1956
Up to this time the Conservation Authorities Act did not apply to any part of Ontario lying within territorial districts. In other words, authorities could be formed

only in the counties of Southern Ontario. This section was repealed making it possible to establish an authority anywhere in Ontario.

One of the most important amendments to the Conservation Authorities Act, also passed in this year, provided for the merger of the four authorities in the Toronto region. These authorities, in order of establishment, were: the Etobicoke River, later enlarged to include Mimico Creek; the Humber River; the Don River; and a group of four small rivers, the Rouge River, Duffin's Creek, Highland Creek and Petticoat Creek, referred as the RDHP.

Singly, each of these authorities had been carrying out projects as far as available funds would permit, but, because of their juxtaposition with the urban centres through which the rivers flowed, it was evident that to carry out a complete conservation programme, the whole area should be dealt with as a unit. Early in 1950 at the request of the Etobicoke authority, a meeting of representatives from the four authorities was held to discuss the merger but no decision was reached. Some of the representatives were not yet ready to forfeit the independence which they enjoyed in managing their own valleys.

In the early 1950s two events took place which emphasized this need and hastened the merger. One was the formation of the municipality of Metropolitan Toronto in 1953, which made it possible for thirteen contiguous municipalities in the Toronto area to join together in carrying out certain important functions. The second was Hurricane Hazel in 1954, which emphasized the necessity of a coordinated flood-control and water-conservation plan for the whole region.

Shortly after Hurricane Hazel, the Honourable W.K. Warrender, planning minister at the time, called another meeting to discuss a merger and invited Frederick G. Gardiner, chairman of Metropolitan Toronto, to attend. During this meeting Mr Gardiner stated that if the merger were carried out with Metropolitan Toronto included, the levy for funds should be based on population which would mean that Metro would be expected to contribute about 92 percent of the total; in that case, Gardiner said, Metro should have representation on the authority equal to all the other municipalities combined. No decision was taken to proceed with the merger.

On 17 August 1955, the Honourable W.M. Nickle was appointed minister of planning. When reviewing with him the work and needs of the authorities, the merger of the four Toronto authorities was brought to his attention and it was pointed out that the situation had reached a stalemate. Mr Nickle was instrumental in having the act amended during the session of the 1956 legislature which brought the merger into being. The name decided on was the Metropolitan Toronto and Region Conservation Authority and the date of establishment was 1 February 1957. Twenty-three municipalities were included of which Metro was by far the largest; the others, usually referred to as rural municipalities, included the remaining towns, villages and townships. The new authority embraced all the land surface in the former four authorities, to which Toronto Island was added, and later, in 1959 when Carruthers Creek was added, the total land surface reached approximately 1,000 square miles.

In discussion of the amendment with officials in the attorney-general's depart-ment, several names for the authority were considered, but none of them – except that chosen – adequately described the area. Unfortunately the name has often been shortened to Metro authority which is misleading because, when used, it suggests a department of Metro Toronto. In recent years, however, many have followed the practice of shortening it to MTRCA.

It should be mentioned also that feelings of local loyalty were taken care of by including in the amendment four watershed advisory boards named after each of the former authorities. (When the act was revised in 1968 this amendment was deleted.) Finally, the suggestion made by Mr Gardiner was included with the result that the number of members from Metropolitan Toronto 'shall at all times be equal to the total number of members appointed by other participating municipalities.'

When the merger was settled, the chairmen and vice-chairmen of the four authorities held a series of meetings to plan the transition of the old into the new. Besides discussing the obvious problems such as office space, technical and office staff and other matters, it was urgent that a capable secretary-treasurer be secured who could be office manager and expedite the business of the authority.

For this position the committee recommended Fred L. Lunn of Brampton. Mr Lunn was a young man who had served six-and-one-half years in the Canadian army overseas in World War II, retiring as a captain. In 1946 he had accepted the position of chief health inspector for Peel County and in 1949, when the Etobicoke authority was formed, was appointed secretary-treasurer. During the ensuing years, the authority built the million dollar flood-control channel in Brampton and the flood-amelioration works in Long Branch. In these two projects as well as other concerns of the authority Mr Lunn became well acquainted with the administration of authorities and carried out his duties with exactitude and enthusiasm.

For the first time the government decided to exercise its prerogative under the act to appoint the chairman of an authority. Accordingly the committee submitted a list of candidates for this office. This list was forwarded to the minister, but to the regret of the committee, no name on the list was acceptable. Other persons were recommended but time went on and no appointment was made. The first of February came and went. It was imperative that a chairman be appointed so that the authority could function, and it was extremely important that a budget be prepared which should be submitted for approval to all member municipalities. It was doubly important that this should be done before the municipalities passed their own budgets. The urgency of this matter was brought to the attention of the minister and in order to expedite matters the author of this study was appointed chairman by order-in-council for one year.

The first meeting of the Metropolitan Toronto and Region Conservation Author-ity was held in the municipal chambers of North York Township on 20 February 1957. At this meeting the vice-chairman was elected, the advisory boards were appointed, the chairmen of which automatically became members of the executive committee. These were: vice-chairman, Eric W. Baker; watersheds advisory boards chairmen: Etobicoke-Mimico – H.M. Griggs; Humber – Dr J.W. Kucherepa; Don – H.S. Honsberger; RDHP – C.R. Purcell. Functional advisory boards chairmen: conservation areas – Charles Sauriol; reforestation and land use – D.J. Redington; information and education – W.S. MacDonnell; historical sites – Mrs Dorothy Hague. Following the elections the executive committee was instructed to prepare a budget for the current year to be presented to the authority at a future meeting.

The second meeting of the authority was held at the same place on 28 February 1957. At this meeting Fred Lunn was appointed secretary-treasurer, the necessary staff was engaged and the budget was adopted.

The first year was a busy one, and much was accomplished. In reading again the annual report of 1957 it is pleasant to discover how many ideas were seeded in that first year, ideas which during the interval have blossomed and brought forth fruit far beyond the most sanguine expectations.

At the first annual meeting held in the council chambers of Vaughan Township, 7 February 1958 the new chairman, Dr G. Ross Lord, professor and head of the department of mechanical engineering at the University of Toronto, was installed. Dr Lord was not a newcomer in the field of conservation; when the staff of the Conservation Branch was first appointed in 1945 he was included as consultant in hydraulic engineering. He had retained this appointment throughout the years, had become imbued with the new philosophy of conservation, and was well informed in the work of conservation authorities.

Also in 1956, the act was amended to permit an authority to make regulations to restrict and regulate the use of water from streams and other natural sources. This amendment was requested by the Big Creek region authority during the time that Evans Knowles was chairman. The need was due to the excessive use of water by tobacco growers in the area during the dry summer of 1955. However, before the authority had time to organize for the implementation of the amendment, the Ontario Water Resources Commission was formed and became responsible for such water problems.

And finally, in that year, the first amendment was passed prohibiting or regulating the dumping of fill of any kind in any area below the high water mark of any river, creek or stream. This amendment was strengthened in 1960–61.

1960

An amendment was passed which provided for the appointment of three members to each authority by the Ontario government. There was much objection to this amendment, especially from the small authorities. The objections were two-fold. The first was that when the act was first passed in 1946 it provided that the government, if it wished, could appoint the chairman of an authority, the chairman of the executive, and one member. From 1946 to 1960 only three appointments were made. The first was in 1947 when Fred Bowen, who had been chairman of the Ganaraska board before the act was passed, was appointed for services rendered; the second was H.R.S. Ryan, the first chairman of the Ganaraska authority as an honorary member; and the third was the appointment of the chairman of the Metropolitan Toronto and Region Conservation Authority in 1957. In these fourteen years the programmes and policies were hammered out solely by the municipal representatives.

The second objection was that the government-appointed members, who were not responsible to municipalities, could vote on equal terms with the other members. If one considers the case of, say, the Catfish Authority with only six members, one sees that the three government members could call a meeting and pass by-laws without consulting the municipal members. This would be defeating the principle on which the authorities were based. In 1968, when the new act was passed, this clause was corrected.

1965

The legislature of Ontario appointed a select committee on conservation authorities 'to enquire into and review the provisions of the Conservation Authorities Act and such other acts of the legislature relevant to the powers exercised by conservation authorities as the committee may deem appropriate.' The committee included 13 members of the legislature, one of whom, D. Arthur Evans, was chairman with H.G. Hooke as technical adviser and Mrs H.G. Rowan as secretary. It commenced its work in 1965 and submitted an interim report in 1966, at which time it was re-appointed with the same terms of reference. The final report of 135 pages was published in 1967 and contained 127 recommendations. Within twelve months more than 100 of the recommendations were implemented.

In 1965 also, a special section was added to the Conservation Authorities Act covering the city of Hamilton and giving it the same proportionate representation on the authority which Metropolitan Toronto enjoyed on the Metropolitan Toronto and Region Conservation Authority. At the same time the Spencer Creek Conservation Authority was enlarged to include Hamilton and the name changed to the Hamilton Region Conservation Authority.

1966

The Grand River Conservation Commission, established in 1938, and the Grand Valley Conservation Authority, established in 1948, were amalgamated under the chairmanship of J.S. Bauer, who had been a member of both the authority and the commission.

Over the years several people had asked why there should be two conservation groups operating in the Grand River watershed. The reason, mentioned briefly in an early chapter, was that the commission was composed of representatives of eight urban municipalities and its work was limited to flood control and increasing summer flow in the river. On the other hand, an authority had power under the act to carry out a multiplicity of conservation projects anywhere on the watershed, was composed of representatives of all the municipalities, cities, towns, villages and townships and was eligible for grants for its projects from the province of Ontario. It is interesting to recall that those who promoted the authority in 1948 were also prominent in the commission. E.F. Roberts, a civil engineer, who was secretary-treasurer of the commission for many years and later chairman, was foremost among those who took part in the venture. And when the authority was formed, William Philip, a retired banker living in Galt who was chairman of the commission was elected chairman of the authority.

The Honourable Dana Porter, planning minister, had some reservations about two groups carrying on conservation on the Grand watershed. He agreed to the establishing of the authority with the provision that when the Conestoga Dam and reservoir, under discussion at that time by the commission, should be completed, the commission would be amalgamated with the authority; however, when that time arrived, Mr Porter had moved on to other duties. In 1962 the Honourable J.W. Spooner had plans for bringing about the amalgamation but he too moved on to other responsibilities and unfortunately the merger was not accomplished until 1966 under the aegis of the Honourable J.R. Simonett.

1968

In this year a number of changes in legislation and administrative procedures were made, based on the recommendations of the select committee on conservation authorities which were of direct concern to the conservation authorities. Most important was the complete rewriting of previous legislation governing authorities in the Conservation Authorities Act 1968. Some of the changes were simply in the nature of housekeeping, since the previous act had been frequently changed by amendments over twenty-two years. Other changes were the result of representations made by the authorities or of recommendations in the report of the select committee on conservation authorities.

'Administration' was redefined so that conservation services were treated as capital projects. The Grand River Conservation Authority was brought under the Conservation Authorities Act 1968. Members were appointed for a fixed term and provisions were made requiring administrative regulations and a minimum number of authority meetings each year. The minister was given emergency powers over water-control structures, the power to approve construction by a conservation authority of works on a lake or river, and wider powers in the making of grants. The authorities' application to the Ontario Municipal Board for financing was made to be an application on behalf of the municipalities. Provision was made for reassessment of authority lands.

A further amendment to the act, presented to the legislature in 1970, facilitates the regulation of changes in stream channels and provides for regional municipalities to become participating municipalities in conservation authorities.

The introduction of regional government has been of some concern to the conservation authorities, which feared that the concept of organization on a watershed basis might be overlooked and that the authorities might be considered just another unnecessary special-purpose body. A reassurance on this point was given by the Honourable W. Darcy McKeough, then minister of municipal affairs, in his comments on the speech from the throne of 2 December 1968:

Conservation: It may prove impossible to integrate the conservation authorities completely within a regional government system. The problem is that conservation authorities must use watershed boundaries reflecting their very specialized role. If a conservation authority is entirely within a regional government we might consider the possibility of making the authority directly responsible to the regional government council, or perhaps making the authority a special committee of council. If, as will often be the case, the conservation authority has boundaries covering all or parts of two or more regional governments, munici-pal representation on the conservation authority governing body, perhaps, should be from the regional government.

Other legislation affecting the authorities was contained in the Expropriations Act 1968–69, which was passed in December 1968. Under this act all expropriating bodies must be prepared to justify their need for expropriation before an inquiry officer. The final decision as to whether or not a conservation authority may expropriate land is now in the hands of the minister and this decision is made after considering a report of any hearing which may be necessary.

To assist authorities with changes in procedure arising from new legislation, the manual of information for conservation authorities has again been completely revised and re-issued to all authorities.

The Conservation Authorities Act 1968, Section 38 provides that, 'Grants may be made by the minister to any authority out of moneys appropriated therefore by the legislature in accordance with such conditions and procedures as may be prescribed by the lieutenant-governor in council.'

The making of such grants is a matter of policy on the part of the government and is subject to change from time to time. For example, when the first flood-control projects were planned – the channel improvement on the Ausable, the Ingersoll flood channel on the Thames and the Brampton flood channel on the Etobicoke – it was anticipated that the government of Canada would contribute 37.5 percent, the government of Ontario 37.5 percent, and the authority 25 percent. Representation was made to Ottawa for such assistance but was denied on all three. Accordingly, as these were the first flood-control projects proposed under the new act and it was important that this new venture be carried through, the Ontario government agreed to underwrite the federal government's share, thereby paying 75 percent of the cost.

During the 1950s two large dams – the Fanshawe on the upper Thames and the Conestoga on the Grand – in the $5 million bracket, were built with 37.5 percent assistance from Canada and Ontario and 25 percent from the authority and commis-sion. While the federal government did not state its policy in writing it was assumed that the only structures which would qualify for federal assistance thereafter must be in the above monetary bracket or greater. This meant that without the assistance from Ottawa grants for flood control for the authorities from Ontario would be 37.5 percent. As a result of this policy there were few small reservoirs built during those years. In 1955 when the Honourable W.M. Nickle became minister of planning and development he was instrumental in having the grants for flood-control projects raised to 50 percent, with no limit on the cost of the structure until it reached an amount to which the federal government might agree to contribute, at which point the Ontario grants reverted to 37.5 percent. But this increase to 50 percent was not sufficient to allow the authorities to build the number of small reservoirs which were needed. However this important problem was solved by the Honourable J.R. Simonett, minister of the department at that time, when in April 1964 he introduced a new policy known as the water supply reservoirs programme.

The new policy [the preamble states] has made provincial assistance available to authorities in the form of a grant of up to 100 percent of the cost of a dam or reservoir including the necessary land acquisition. Twenty-five percent of the grant must be paid by the authority within thirteen years after initiation of the project. The first three years of the repayment period are interest free. The remainder may be repaid any time during the ten years and bears interest at a specified rate.

The schedule of grants to authorities, 1970, which follows, will indicate how policy has changed over the years since the first grants were made for flood control and reforestation.

SCHEDULE OF GRANTS TO AUTHORITIES, 1970

Administration as defined in Section 1(a) of the Conservation Authorities Act, 1968: 'Administration' costs means salaries and travelling expenses of members and employees of an authority, office rent, maintenance and purchase of office equipment, expenses connected with exhibits, visual equipment and printed matter for educational purposes, and all expenses necessary for carrying out the objects of an authority other than capital expenses and maintenance costs of approved projects	Ontario Authority	50% 50%
Preliminary engineering studies, surveys for hydraulic projects	Ontario Authority	75% 25%
The policy for large dams and reservoirs which were financed in previous years by Canada 37.5 percent, Ontario 37.5 percent and Authority 25 percent is not expected to be continued but the agreements of the upper Thames and the Metropolitan Toronto and Region Conservation Authorities whose ten year-period has run out will be extended until the original funds agreed to are used up. Acquisition of land for forestry, (authority forests), wildlife areas, wet land and water conservation under the Agricultural Rehabilitation and Development Act 1961 Canada	ARDA Ontario Authority	37¹/₂% 37¹/₂% 25%
Dams and reservoirs other than those built under the water supply reservoirs programme	Ontario Authority	50% 50%
Dams and Reservoirs built under the water supply reservoirs programme	Ontario Authority	75% 25%

Flood control channels, river bank erosion and miscellaneous other hydraulic projects	Ontario	50%
	Authority	50%
Maintenance on dams and certain water control structures only	Ontario	75%
	Authority	25%
Flood plain mapping	Ontario	75%
	Authority	25%
Acquisition of flood plain land	Ontario	50%
	Authority	50%
Acquisition of land for conservation areas	Ontario	50%
	Authority	50%
Acquisition of Niagara escarpment land for conservation areas	Ontario	75%
	Authority	25%

Epilogue

As Dr Richardson has demonstrated, the conservation authority movement has been a movement of, by, and for the people; so it began and so it has continued for a quarter of a century. When people contribute directly to an authority's work, whether in taxes or in a freely given donation of time and service, they take a personal – and, often, a proprietary – interest in the projects; the dam becomes '*my* dam,' the forest becomes '*my* forest.' If the movement is removed from this close relationship with the people it serves there is a danger to the future of the Ontario conservation authorities.

Governments grow and expand. Within the last few years 'regional' governments have been established in several parts of the province, a step which may make for efficiency but certainly interposes another level of administration between the governed and their government. And within governments, the number of departments, services, and ministries multiplies alarmingly. Should the conservation authorities, particularly the small authorities, abrogate their responsibilities, governments will assume them. When government takes over, the personal and proprietary interest of the citizen is lost.

The provincial government has already taken over two programmes initiated by conservation authorities – the farm pond and tree-planting programmes mentioned in Dr Richardson's text. In these two instances, perhaps, there was some justification for governmental control inasmuch as the conservation authorities do not cover all the watersheds of Ontario.

If the conservation authorities movement is to continue to be as effective for the next twenty-five years it must remain a cooperative venture between local municipalities and the provincial government, ably supported by the voluntary efforts of individual conservationists and organizations such as the Nature Conservancy of Canada.

In addition, every effort must be made to establish authorities on every watershed particularly in populated areas. Small authorities must be amalgamated

– the upper and lower Thames River authorities must be combined and a single authority be established on the Trent watershed.

If these steps are taken, the historian who writes the history of the next twenty-five years will be able to describe a record of achievement even greater than that outlined by Dr Richardson.

A.S.L. BARNES

APPENDIXES AND INDEX

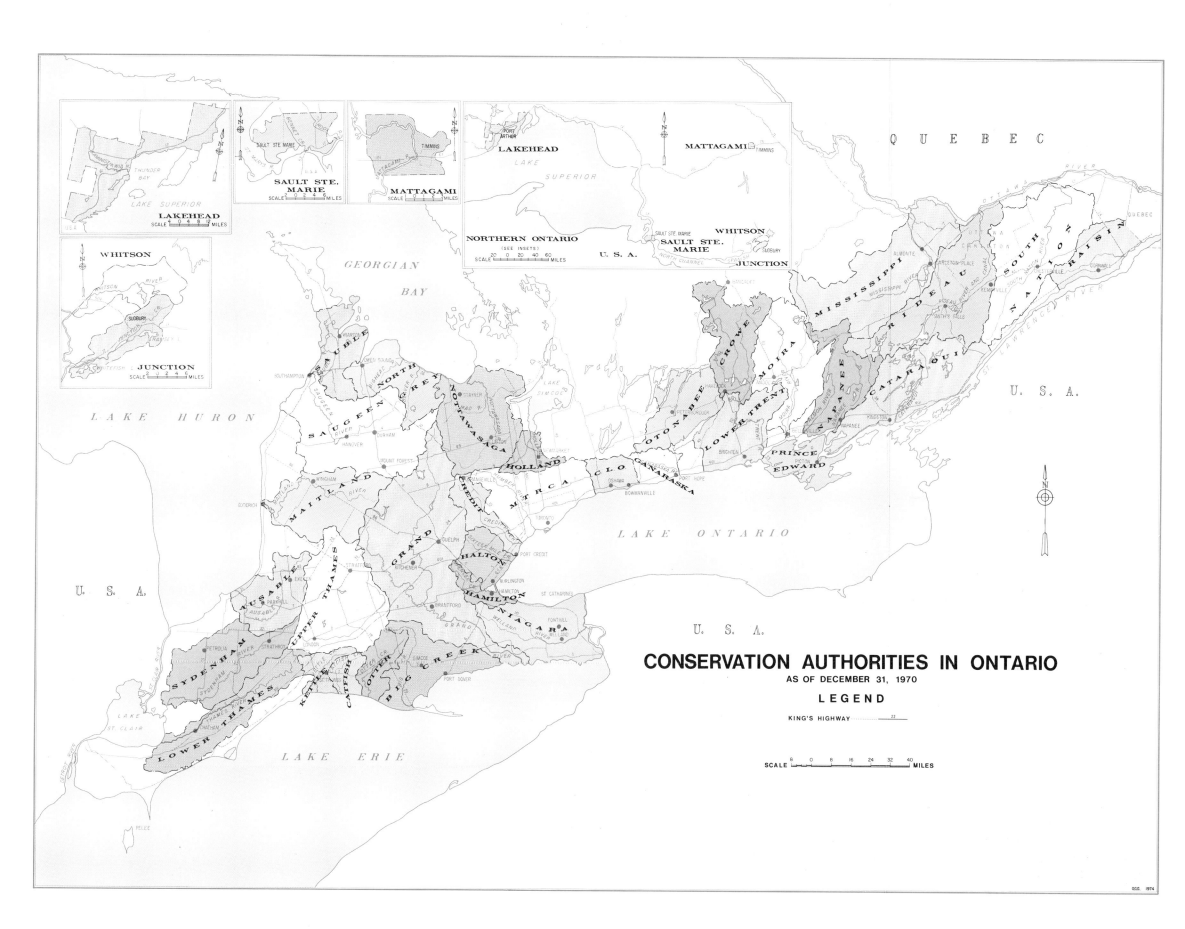

CONSERVATION AUTHORITIES IN ONTARIO

AS OF DECEMBER 31, 1970

LEGEND

KING'S HIGHWAY · · · · · · · · · · ·

SCALE | 8 0 8 16 24 32 40 | MILES

Appendix A

Conservation Authorities in order of establishment
to 31 December 1970

ORIGINAL CONSERVATION AUTHORITY	DATE OF ESTABLISHMENT	ENLARGEMENTS & CHANGES OF NAME
Ausable River	30 July 1946	
Etobicoke River	30 July 1946	Enlarged Etobicoke-Mimico 1 December 1949. Amalgamated MTRCA 1 February 1967
Ganaraska River	8 October 1946	Enlarged Ganaraska Region 15 March 1962, 16 July 1970
South Nation River	8 May 1947	
Moira River	31 July 1947	
Upper Thames River	18 September 1947	Enlarged 6 May 1954
Napanee Valley	20 November 1947	Enlarged Napanee Region 8 July 1965
Big Creek Valley (after 1970, became Long Point)	9 September 1948	Enlarged Big Creek Region 5 August 1954, Enlarged 2 January 1969
Grand Valley	26 February 1948	Became Grand River on 6 April 1966, enlarged 28 November 1968
Don Valley	29 April 1948	Amalgamated in MTRCA 1 February 1957
Humber Valley	29 April 1948	Amalgamated in MTRCA 1 February 1957
Catfish Creek	23 February 1950	Enlarged 29 March 1961
Saugeen Valley	16 March 1950	Enlarged 27 May 1954
Upper Holland Valley (after 1970, became South Lake Simcoe)	6 September 1951	Enlarged Holland Valley 24 March 1960
Middle Maitland Valley	6 September 1951	Enlarged Maitland Valley 16 November 1961

ORIGINAL CONSERVATION AUTHORITY	DATE OF ESTABLISHMENT	ENLARGEMENTS & CHANGES OF NAME
Rouge, Duffin, Highland and Petticoat (RDHP)	1 April 1954 Amended 2 April 1954	Amalgamated in MTRCA 1 February 1957
Credit Valley	13 May 1954	Enlarged 17 February 1955 (Joshua Creek to Sixteen-Mile 17 April 1963)
Neebing Valley	15 July 1954	Enlarged Lakehead Region 1 January 1963
Otter Creek (after 1970, became part of Long Point)	5 August 1954	Enlarged 2 February 1956 Enlarged 29 March 1961
Sixteen-Mile Creek	20 December 1956	Enlarged (Joshua) 17 April 1963 Amalgamated in Halton Region 30 December 1963
Metropolitan Toronto and Region	1 February 1957	
North Grey Region	5 June 1957	
Junction Creek (after 1970, became Nickel District)	12 December 1957	Enlarged 1 January 1970
Spencer Creek	8 May 1958	Enlarged to Hamilton Region 1 June 1966
Twelve-Mile Creek	12 June 1958	Enlarged 1 August 1963 Amalgamated into Halton Region 30 December 1963
Central Lake Ontario	17 July 1958	
Sauble Valley	17 July 1958	Enlarged 3 September 1959 Enlarged 14 March 1963
Crowe Valley	6 November 1958	
Niagara Peninsula	30 April 1959	
Otonabee Valley	9 July 1959	Enlarged (Indian River) to the Otonabee Region 24 March 1960, Enlarged (Ouse) 29 March 1961, Enlarged (Ennismore Twp.) 13 March 1969
Whitson Valley (after 1970, became part of Nickel District)	3 September 1959	
Holland Valley	24 March 1960	
Nottawasaga Valley	5 May 1960	
Sydenham Valley	12 January 1961	
Lower Thames Valley	2 February 1961	Enlarged 19 May 1966 and 19 September 1968
Maitland Valley	16 November 1961	
Mattagami Valley	30 November 1961	
Lakehead Region	1 January 1963	
Raisin River	10 October 1963	Enlarged to Raisin Region 29 February 1968
Sault Ste Marie Region	21 November 1963	
Halton Region	30 December 1963	
Cataraqui Region	17 December 1964	

ORIGINAL CONSERVATION AUTHORITY	DATE OF ESTABLISHMENT	ENLARGEMENTS & CHANGES OF NAME
Kettle Creek	1 April 1965	
Prince Edward Region	16 December 1965	
Hamilton Region	1 June 1966	Enlarged from Spencer Creek 16 March 1966
Rideau Valley	31 March 1966	
Mississippi Valley	2 May 1968	
Lower Trent	16 May 1968	

Appendix B

CHRONOLOGY OF THE BRANCH – 1944–1970

Department		*Minister*		*Deputy Minister*	
Conservation Branch – A.H. Richardson, director, 1944 to 30 Nov. 1961					
Planning and					
Development	1944–1960	Dana Porter	1944–1948	G.B. Langford	
				Director of Department	1944–1946
		G. Arthur Welsh	1948–1950	None	
		Wm. Griesinger	1950–1953	None	
		Wm. Warrender	1953–1955	None	
		W.M. Nickle	1955–1960	T.A.C. Tyrell	1957–1960
Commerce and					
Development	1960–1961	W.M. Nickle	1960–1961	T.A.C. Tyrell	1960–1961
Economics and					
Development	1961	W.M. Nickle	Oct.–Nov. 1961	T.A.C. Tyrell	1961
		R.W. Macaulay	Nov.–Dec. 1961	S.W. Clarkson	1961
Conservation Authorities Branch – A.S.L. Barnes, director, 1961 – 1970					
Lands & Forests	1962–1964	J.W. Spooner	Jan.–Oct. 1962	F.A. MacDougall	1962–1964
		A. Kelso Roberts	1962–1964		
Energy and Resources		J.R. Simonett	1964–1969	R.D. Hilliard	1964–1966
Management	1964–1970	G.A. Kerr	1969–1970	J.C. Thatcher	1966–1970

Index